With Bound Hands

With
BOUND HANDS

A JESUIT IN NAZI GERMANY

The Life and
Selected Prison Letters of
Alfred Delp

MARY FRANCES COADY

an imprint of
LOYOLAPRESS.
CHICAGO

JESUIT WAY

an imprint of

LOYOLAPRESS.

3441 N. ASHLAND AVENUE
CHICAGO, ILLINOIS 60657
(800) 621-1008
WWW.LOYOLABOOKS.ORG

Library of Congress Cataloging-in-Publication Data

Coady, Mary Frances.
    With bound hands : a Jesuit in Nazi Germany : the life and selected prison letters of Alfred Delp / Mary Frances Coady.
        p.   cm.
Includes bibliographical references (p.   ) and index.
    ISBN 0-8294-1794-X
    1. Delp, Alfred.   2. Jesuits—Germany—Biography.   I. Delp, Alfred. Correspondence. English. Selections.   II. Title.
    BX4705.D422C63 2003
    271'.5302—dc21

                                                                2003008149

Printed in the United States of America
03 04 05 06 07 08 09 10 Bang 10 9 8 7 6 5 4 3 2 1

*. . . unless a grain of wheat falls into
the earth and dies, it remains just a single grain;
but if it dies, it bears much fruit.*
(John 12:24)

CONTENTS

ACKNOWLEDGMENTS

Alfred Delp became well known as a figure of the German resistance with the publication in 1956 of *Im Angesicht des Todes* (In the Face of Death), a selection of writings that were smuggled out of prison during the months before his execution. The English translation appeared in North America in 1963, with an introduction by Thomas Merton, under the title *The Prison Meditations of Father Alfred Delp* (Herder and Herder).

Among the writings in that work was a section with the heading "Excerpts from Father Delp's Diary." In fact, Delp did not keep a diary in prison; the writings in this section were smuggled out as letters "To M." In the present book, these letters have been restored to their original form. This book also contains a selection of the prison letters Delp wrote to friends and family members. These letters, along with most of Delp's other prison writings, were published in 1984 in volume 4 of *Gesammelte Schriften,* edited by Roman Bleistein.

Several people have assisted me with offers of ideas and suggestions, help with historical context and translation, and general encouragement. In particular, I'm indebted to Haide Aide, Jörg Dantscher, S.J., Mario Galeazzi, Pat Halpin, F.C.J., Margaret

Holubowich, Tibor Horvath, S.J., Margot King, Gertrud Jaron Lewis, Peter Schmidt, O.C.S.O., and Wiebke Smythe.

For much help and gracious hospitality I'm grateful in a special way to Peter Hammerich, parish priest of St. Andreas Church in Lampertheim; to Hans-Georg Lachmund, S.J.; and to Sister Maria-Theresia and the community of Karmel Regina Martyrum in Berlin.

I'm also grateful to Philip Endean, S.J., for generously sharing with me some of his work on Alfred Delp. And to Dr. Rita Haub, archivist of the Upper German Province of the Society of Jesus, for her help and cooperation.

It was a particular privilege to spend some brief time with people who knew Alfred Delp personally, and I thank them for relating their memories of him: Karl-Adolph Kreuser, S.J., the son of his good friends; Otto Ogiermann, S.J., and Richard Wagner, S.J., his contemporaries; Freya von Moltke, widow of Helmuth von Moltke and woman of extraordinary courage; Marianne (Kern) Junk, Delp's niece; and Fritz Delp, his brother.

Many thanks to Jim Manney, Matthew Diener, and all at Loyola Press who have seen this book through to completion.

Finally, I want to acknowledge the help of the late Roman Bleistein, S.J., who extended a courteous welcome when I arrived unannounced at the door of Alfred Delp Haus in Munich one day in the spring of 1994 and who continued to provide helpful information up until two months before his death in August 2000. Roman Bleistein wrote extensively on Jesuit activity during the period of the Third Reich. Thanks to his meticulous work, the drama and complexity of Alfred Delp's life have been saved from obscurity, and as a result, Delp's spiritual legacy has emerged all the more rich and profound.

PROLOGUE

There are four existing photos of the Jesuit Alfred Delp from his trial for high treason on January 9 and 10, 1945, before the People's Court of Germany's Third Reich. In one photo, the thirty-seven-year-old priest stands with his square jaw thrust upward, his hands extended, his fingertips together as if trying to make a clear and reasoned point. He wears a business suit with a shirt and tie. There is animation, and even defiance, in his stance. His physique appears strong and reveals no signs of the six-month ordeal he has just been through: nine weeks of interrogation as well as beatings and psychological pressure to abandon the Jesuits for the Nazis, followed by four months of solitary confinement. He emanates confidence, or so it seems. He has always been loyal to the highest ideal: justice for all humanity under God's law. No evidence links him to the July 20, 1944, attempt on German Chancellor Adolf Hitler's life, which was the purported reason for his arrest.

Through high windows, broad daylight fills the courtroom. Stoic-looking guards in Prussian helmets flank Delp. Behind him sits the lanky Protestant nobleman-lawyer Helmuth von Moltke, also on trial, whose vision of a German constitution based on Christian social principles launched the resistance group known as the Kreisau

Circle. Since Delp joined the group three years ago, the two have become good friends. Religious differences have paled in the light of their common ideal of a renewed society. It will soon become clear that Moltke's fate has been decided by his association with Jesuits.

In the second photo, Delp is looking down, with his eyeglasses a bit askew, his thick hair on the verge of becoming unkempt. The camera has caught his hands in an awkward clasp, as if he is unsure of himself, as if he has become speechless. Perhaps at this point he realizes that the trial is a sham, a mere showpiece for the red-robed judge, Roland Freisler, to win points with Hitler. Perhaps this photo captures the moment when Freisler points a derisive finger at Delp, his dark eyebrows raised in fury, and half-rising from his chair, shrieks, "You miserable creep! You clerical nobody." Perhaps it is now clear that the careful preparation for this day—the secret strategizing, the clandestine notes, the anxious straining toward a favorable outcome—was all for nothing. The People's Court, filled with Nazis to give the impression of a normal judicial procedure, is nothing but a means to parade and humiliate the accused in front of the camera (on Hitler's orders) before condemning them to death.

The third and fourth pictures are a bit blurry. Delp is gazing downward, alone, slack-jawed, perhaps immobilized by the icy realization of his fate. For this is what it has come to: the clever young Jesuit, so hopeful for the outcome of this trial, is to be executed, by hanging, as an enemy of the state.

It is not clear when the death sentence will be carried out. Delp is driven back to Berlin's Tegel Prison, his hands again fettered, as they have been for all these months. The steel door of his cell clangs shut behind him, and the turning key fixes the bolt with a thud. Days pass slowly, the damp January cold seeping through the barred window of his narrow cell.

Perhaps there will be a reprieve, though it is unlikely. It has become widely known that the days of the Third Reich are numbered, that the people are demoralized and numb with exhaustion, that the country lies in ruins, but the Nazis are now lashing out wherever they can in brutal acts of desperation. Perhaps an Allied Forces bomb will fall on the prison—they have been falling nightly across Germany—and in the chaos the prisoners will escape. Or best of all: perhaps the Russian troops making their way west toward Berlin will soon bring liberation. Each day of life is precious, despite the damp cold and loneliness, the uncertainty and fear.

On January 23 word reaches Delp that Moltke and other members of the Kreisau Circle have been executed. Why them and not him? Does God have some grand plan that will see him walk out the prison's front door a free man? These months in captivity have done much to purify him, and have given him new insight, new sensitivities. The barred window, the fettered hands, and the narrow cell door that can open only from the outside—these have become his teacher, his mentor, his spiritual director. He has wrestled with God, over and over again, falling close to despair at times. All his securities and his life's promise have crumbled: his stature as an intellectual, his talent for writing and preaching, his political ideas, and his vision for a better society. Perhaps these newly discovered insights are a sign that God has special plans for him.

January drags on toward its dreary end. Delp's taut nerves have brought him close to the breaking point, yet with each new day, there is hope of liberation.

But then, on the last day of January, the door of Delp's cell is opened and he is led to a car and then driven to Plötzensee Prison, a short distance away. There, he is led through the front door, across the broad courtyard, and into the cellblock known as the House of the Dead. He is handed the striped uniform of the condemned prisoner and a sheet of paper that lists the articles of clothing he is leaving behind. He signs the paper with a shaking hand and dons the prison garb. All he has left of his own now is a rosary. At his request, he is brought a copy of Thomas à Kempis's *The Imitation of Christ.*

"Nor is there any remedy or means of escape from ills and griefs; you must endure them. Drink lovingly of the cup of your Lord, if you wish to be his friend."[1]

And now it is Friday, February 2, the Feast of the Purification of Mary. "Next week the First Friday, special to the Sacred Heart, and a Marian feast are on the same day," he wrote to a friend several days ago. "Please pray."[2] At Tegel Prison, a system devised by the chaplain and two social workers allowed Delp to have letters smuggled in and out with the laundry. Here, in the House of the Dead, no such system exists, and it is probably just as well. He has written his farewells, and there is nothing left to say. All that remains now is to face God. Between the time he signed over his clothes in emotional distress and the chaplain's final visit just before he is led away, a peace has settled upon him. "In half an hour, I'll know more than you do," he tells the chaplain with a smile.[3]

Just before three o'clock on this Friday afternoon—is he aware at this point of the significance of the time and the day?—a guard unlocks his cell. Delp takes off his eyeglasses and leaves them on the small table beside his rosary and *The Imitation of Christ.* He is led through a series of doors into a courtyard, and then to a small one-story brick building. Inside, the building is one cavernous room with a cement floor. A black curtain has been pulled across the width of the room. An official stands before him and reads out the verdict of the People's Court. The priest Alfred Delp is condemned to death by hanging as an enemy of the state. The black curtain is pulled away, and ahead, at the top of the chamber, in front of two rounded windows, he sees eight meat hooks hanging from the ceiling. He is led toward one of them.

———

In the years after his death, Alfred Delp's classmates from his early years in the Society of Jesus were to remember him as an enfant terrible. He was a maverick, and at times a Jesuit superior's headache. "He lived as a sinner and died as a martyr" became a saying among them.

"Don't let my mother tell any 'pious legends' about me," he wrote to a friend from prison. "I was a brat."[4] Indeed, even his entry into the world, on September 15, 1907, took place under irregular circumstances. . . .

CHAPTER I

YOUNG SCAMP

1907–1926

Like most of the crowned monarchs in Europe, Kaiser Wilhelm II of Germany was ruling his country with an uncertain hand when, on the Feast of Our Lady of Sorrows, in the southern city of Mannheim, Maria Bernauer held for the first time her tiny, bundled, newborn son.

The twenty-six-year-old kitchen worker was likely not aware when she gave her baby the kingly name of Alfred that the great imperial systems were crumbling and that stirrings of unrest would explode into war in just a few years. Even if she had been aware, it would not have mattered at that moment. There were more immediate questions on her mind as she gazed down at her sleeping infant, with one question above all: Would the baby's father marry her now?

They were, after all, a family of sorts. This was already their second child; the first, Justina, had been born two years earlier and had been given to Maria's married, childless sister to raise. She did not want to give up her son as well. As the unmarried mother of two children, Maria was in an unusual situation for a young woman of pious Catholic peasant stock. One wonders what combination of passion and rebellion led her to push against the mores of the times, the expected standards of respectability, and the disapproval of the Church and its threat of eternal damnation.

And what of the hesitant father? Friedrich Delp's status as an office worker placed him a notch above Maria on the social scale, and this class distinction may have played a role in his unwillingness to marry her. But probably more significant, he was a Lutheran. Passion, rebellion, ecumenism by default, a whiff of the outcast: it was an auspicious start in life for the young Alfred.

Perhaps it was the birth of a son that finally made the reluctant Friedrich decide to overcome religious differences and take responsibility for his family. In any case, he married Maria a month later, and by that event the baby's birth was legitimized. Eventually, Alfred was joined by two more sisters, Gerda and Greta, and two brothers, Ewald and Fritz.

In 1914 the Delp family moved to the town of Lampertheim, south of Frankfurt, near the Rhine River. They lived in three rooms above a restaurant that was situated a few steps from the Catholic church of St. Andreas, a modest white building with a medieval bell tower. Directly across the street stood the imposing brick of St. Luke's Lutheran church. At his father's insistence, the young Alfred, though baptized a Catholic, attended the Lutheran school and received religious instruction there.

The high-spirited youngster became a scamp and a troublemaker but was clever and original in his ability to avoid punishment. He sometimes fished in forbidden streams and, when caught, used his younger sister as a foil, allowing her innocence to appease authority. As he grew older, he seemed just as keen about reading books as he was about getting into trouble. His siblings remembered that sometimes after reading he would sit alone quietly in a corner, thinking about what he had just read. He was a bright student and soon proved a promising Evangelical scholar.

He seems to have been equally at home at St. Andreas, however, and became friendly with Father Johannes Unger, the parish priest.

In March 1921, by now a big-boned youth of thirteen, Alfred was confirmed in the Lutheran church. The story goes that shortly afterward an altercation took place between the pastor and the headstrong teenager. When he arrived late to a religion lesson one day, Alfred was asked by the pastor to explain himself. He replied that he had been with Father Unger. The pastor, perhaps angry at the newly confirmed Lutheran's visit with a Catholic priest or annoyed at what he perceived as an insolent response, slapped the boy across the face. Alfred stormed out of the church, vowed never to return, and crossed the street for St. Andreas in search of Father Unger. This adolescent willfulness marked a turning point in his young life. Father Unger began instructing him in the Catholic faith, and in June he made his first communion and was confirmed in the Catholic Church nine days later.

The following year he entered the minor seminary in Dieburg, a few miles north of Lampertheim, with a vague, youthful notion of studying for the priesthood. This move was the first big change in his life; he moved from the closeness of family life into the world of an institution, with its long corridors and high ceilings, its smells of wood polish and incense and candle wax, the regular ringing of bells, and the explosive physical energy of dozens of other teenage boys. It was also an introduction to the larger world of ideas, of change.

The world he had been born into had changed as well. The material deprivation, such as food shortages, that all Germans had become used to during World War I had not abated to any extent, and there was the more searing humiliation of defeat in war. Soldiers had limped home bloody and disillusioned. The massive reparations mandated by the Treaty of Versailles had brought Germany to its knees. Workers roamed the country in search of

Alfred Delp as a student in Dieburg, at the age of about fifteen. *Courtesy of the Archives of St. Andreas Church, Lampertheim.*

employment. The shaky Weimar Republic had replaced the monarchy. In the wake of the massive political shift, the romantic idea of the Fatherland began to grow popular among German youth. Youth movements burgeoned, inspired more or less by socialist principles—an idealistic desire to improve conditions in the country and restore justice.

Catholic leaders began their own youth movements. German Catholics had wanted to show their patriotism for more than half a century, ever since Otto von Bismarck's Kulturkampf movement in the 1870s had closed down churches and religious houses in an attempt to drive Catholicism out of Germany. The idea behind the Catholic youth movements of the 1920s was to combine the Catholic social principles laid out in Pope Leo XIII's encyclical *Rerum Novarum* (Of New Things) three decades earlier with a genuine service to the battered Fatherland and a desire to transcend class conflicts and party divisions.

One such group was Neudeutschland, whose idealistic spirit was embodied in its general secretary, the Jesuit Ludwig Esch. Alfred Delp joined Neudeutschland and quickly became a passionate member of the group, participating with high enthusiasm in the rallies and marching songs. He loved the idea of replacing old concepts with fiery new ideas about patriotism and serving God. He soon became a leader in the movement, whistling and calling outside the windows of other youths in the early mornings to rouse them into action for the rallies.

Decision to Join the Jesuits

Back in Lampertheim, Father Unger saw a budding theologian in Alfred and spoke highly of him to the local bishop. On the priest's recommendation, the bishop arranged for the young scholar to attend the Germanicum in Rome, the seminary for the most intellectually promising of the German candidates for the diocesan priesthood. Young Alfred, however, had other ideas. Through his Jesuit contacts in Neudeutschland, he had read about some of the saints who belonged to the Society of Jesus and had gone on a retreat based on St. Ignatius's *Spiritual Exercises*. He wanted to become a Jesuit, but he remained in hesitant silence as plans rolled along for him to travel to Rome and enter the prestigious seminary. Finally, lacking the courage to write to Father Unger to let him know he had changed his mind, he wrote to his mother and asked her to be his messenger. When Maria Delp presented the letter to Father Unger, the priest lamented, "With the Jesuits he'll vegetate somewhere as a prefect of students."[1]

As for why Delp wanted to throw in his lot with the Jesuits, he wrote in answer to the official application question, "I think that I can best serve the Savior there."[2] He gave no further explanation, nor is it known which Jesuits throughout history particularly inspired him. He had plenty of examples to choose from: youthful saints such as Aloysius Gonzaga, distinguished churchmen such as Peter Canisius, and the long list of missionaries and martyrs, from Francis Xavier in the sixteenth century to the Mexican martyr Miguel Pro in the early twentieth century. He certainly would have read the story of Ignatius Loyola, who had founded the Society of Jesus four centuries earlier upon his own military style of life and who had purified his vision of soldiers for Christ in a damp cave in Manresa, Spain. Despite the horrific backdrop of war against which Alfred had lived much of his childhood, as a young teenager he had dreamed of the soldier's life, and the Ignatian military model likely attracted him; indeed, Jesuits had served on both sides during World War I.

The swashbuckling history of the Jesuits may also have been a draw. Over the centuries, the Jesuits had been lauded and vilified, raised up and struck down. They had become the champions of the Counter Reformation and the defenders of the papacy, guarding the fortress of the Roman Catholic Church. As its numbers swelled and its power and influence grew, the Society of Jesus, in fact, developed into a double fortress: an often-reviled organization fending off attacks on itself within the besieged Church.

The Society of Jesus had almost disappeared in the eighteenth century, when for fifty-two years it was suppressed by the Church, but it grew in ever greater numbers after it was reinstated in 1814. But then, as a result of Bismarck's Kulturkampf, many religious orders in Germany, including the Jesuits, were expelled and their institutions closed. The Jesuits, Bismarck claimed, were the scourge of young minds and a danger to society. The bill of expulsion remained on the books until 1917.

Undeterred, however, the Jesuits simply moved outside the German borders and set up new institutions. They opened a novitiate at Tisis, near the town of Feldkirch in western Austria, where there already was a large Jesuit school for boys. The building sat in a wide valley surrounded by mountains. The novitiate at Tisis was where Alfred Delp headed at the age of eighteen, shortly after finishing his school exams.

CHAPTER 2

BECOMING A JESUIT

1926–1937

The young man from Lampertheim who traveled to the Jesuit novitiate in Tisis in the spring of 1926 was tall with an athletic-looking build, though he was poorly co-ordinated and not particularly good at sports. Beneath a thick swatch of light brown hair, combed straight back in an attempt at tidiness, his face appeared angular and square-jawed. The physical impression was one of lopsidedness: thin, black-rimmed glasses sat askew on the bridge of his nose. In repose, his mouth was tightlipped and crooked, his expression intense and serious, suggesting also a tendency toward impatience and perhaps a hint of smoldering anger. When he smiled, his teeth appearing slightly crooked, his face was transformed, and his eyes sparkled. He loved verbal jousting, his voice often erupting into a loud, staccato ha-ha-ha that rose above the laughter around him. Years later, this was what his classmates would remember about him (besides his some-what unusual Lutheran background): his loud, distinctive laugh as well as his raucous singing. He seemed unaware, or perhaps he did not care, that he was incapable of carrying a tune. (Likewise, to the chagrin of his teachers, the handwriting that revealed the working of his sharp mind remained deplorable.)

The neophyte, then, who presented himself at the novitiate door on April 22, 1926, soon to become "Frater Delp", was a compelling mixture of piercing intelligence, high-energy zest for life, and loudmouthed bravado.

He was already used to the all-male institutional hothouse atmosphere in which young men were immersed in the ideals of service to God, but this new venture was a considerable leap. The regimen was one of strict discipline punctuated by bells that he soon learned signified strict religious obedience, one of the cornerstones of Jesuit life. The novices rose every day at five o'clock in the morning (in former days the rising hour had been four, but because many of the novices had come through the war malnourished, an extra hour of sleep was allowed). The environment was austere, the diet drab. The novices developed what they called "monks' knees" from long hours of kneeling in the chapel. They washed in cold water, and the result was less-than-perfect hygiene.

The daily routine included meditation on the life of Christ according to a set Ignatian formula, close examination of conscience, manual work, and exercise, all within an atmosphere of silence. Readings from the lives of the saints or *The Imitation of Christ* accompanied mealtimes. Latin was to be spoken except at specified times, although the purity of the language was badly abused by high-spirited youths who quickly learned that they could create a pseudo-Latin by tacking Latinate noun and verb endings onto their native German. (The theologian Karl Rahner, a young Jesuit at the time, was brought in to give lessons in proper Latin to Delp and the other novices.)

The novices went on regular hiking excursions in the nearby mountains of the Vorarlberg region so they could stretch their limbs and breathe the clear alpine air, but otherwise the schedule remained unchanged. The novitiate's purpose was to set the novice up for an intense relationship with God that would deepen over the course of his life. Here, often struggling with the torpor of early-morning sleepiness, novices learned the exhortations with which Ignatius had trained his followers: to find God in all things and to do all for God's greater glory.

The regimen was in fact a monastic one, and Jesuits often complained that the novitiate prepared them for life in a monastery rather than life in the secular world into which they were to be thrust. Indeed, Delp and his fellow cloistered novices may not even have been aware that while they were following the dull routine of prayer and work, a young Austrian named Adolf Hitler and his fledgling political party had begun making waves in the struggling Weimar Republic across the border.

For Delp, however, the novitiate experience did something else that no other life preparation could have achieved: it placed God at the center of his consciousness. The novitiate, with its steadfast insistence on silence, meditation, and unrelenting reliance on God's will, laid the groundwork for this change in Delp. The meaning of this important shift would gradually become clear to him, especially so in the last six months of his life.

Delp indicated the program he had set for his own life in a poem he wrote a few years later for a fellow Jesuit who was leaving for a mission in India:

> Over vast oceans
> Serve eternity!
> Become there, like Christ,
> A warrior for the kingdom of God.
> Bear with faithful courage
> The Savior's blood everywhere.
> Free human hearts,
> Be a helper and a savior.[1]

Life As a Jesuit Scholastic

In 1928, Delp made his first vows of poverty, chastity, and obedience, and now became a scholastic—a candidate for the priesthood. He was sent first to study philosophy at Berchmanskolleg in Pullach, south of Munich, a facility that had been built in haste a few years earlier to accommodate the large numbers that had been joining the Jesuits. If they had been sequestered from the outside world during the novitiate, the young scholastics were now thrust into that world and into a Church on the edge of radical new thinking.

From the time of the Counter Reformation, Catholic philosophy, which formed the bedrock of the Church's teaching, had been stuck in medieval scholasticism. Radical and dynamic in its time, scholastic philosophy had by the nineteenth century become reductionist and fossilized, a means of holding the Catholic Church together. By the beginning of the twentieth century, scholars were pressing forward in efforts to revitalize Catholic philosophical thinking, to bring it into dialogue with the contemporary world and the ideas of secular thinkers. The Jesuits were at the forefront of the push. The Vatican, which gave the movement the derisive term *modernism,* harshly squelched all tentative forays into new thinking. The English Jesuit George Tyrell, who argued that the Catholic Church, like any other organization, should be open to critical analysis, was expelled from the Society of Jesus because of his writings. Despite his efforts to stay reconciled with the Church, he was excommunicated.

But the bulwark of conformist thinking was beginning, if slowly, to crack. In 1919, the French Jesuit Pierre Teilhard de Chardin, who eventually would come under severe censure himself, wrote from his postwar lodging on the banks of the Rhine River that if Christians had a duty to embrace the Church, the Church had an equal duty to embrace the human race and that the encouragement of ideas was preferable to the propagation of empty rituals. His writing was not widely circulated, but this kind of critical thinking was now in the air; theology schools began to buzz with once unthinkable thoughts about God and the Church. By the late 1920s, Jesuit thinkers such as the Belgian Joseph Maréchal were turning away from a static notion of God in search of a more dynamic philosophy and theology. The work of these thinkers was beginning to inspire dialogue with the intellectual thought of secular philosophy and other disciplines.

Within the official teaching office of the Church itself, a breakthrough had occurred in 1891 with the publication of the encyclical *Rerum Novarum*. Written in the wake of the industrial revolution, this encyclical highlighted the primacy of labor over capital, the needs of the poor and the factory workers, the division of ownership, and the need for the Church to support the aspirations of workers to find meaning in their work. In 1931, Pope Pius XI, in a fortieth-anniversary encyclical, *Quadragesimo Anno* (Fortieth Year), offered a Christian alternative to Communism. All of this new thinking was to take several more decades to mature, but, in the European schools of philosophy and theology, students of Delp's generation reaped the benefits as Catholic social thought took root.

Delp himself was in his element during these years of study: he loved history, especially the history of political change, and he dove into debates on controversial matters with blithe unconcern about others' sensibilities. He showed a particular interest in the new social teaching of the Church and was to become during the 1930s an expert in this field, especially in matters concerning *Quadragesimo Anno.*

These exciting intellectual developments, however, were taking place against an increasingly sinister economic and political backdrop. Declining agricultural prices and the 1929 stock market crash brought extreme poverty to an already suffering Germany. Millions of people were unemployed; as a result, many people tended to move toward one or other of the two extreme parties, the Communist Party and the National Socialist Party. The Jesuits, not unreasonably, feared that a major swing in either direction would mean yet another expulsion for them. In a letter to his brother Ewald just before the September 1930 election, Delp stressed the urgency of a win for the Catholic Center Party, a moderate political party that had been formed to safeguard Catholic rights; otherwise, he wrote, "you can visit your brother in exile in a few years."[2]

As for Delp himself, a complex set of personality traits had begun to manifest itself. He combined a deeply intense prayer life with a manic whirlwind of activity, throwing himself into everything he did—sports, work, study—with enormous vigor. His energy was so extraordinary that he was able to add a major study of the philosopher Martin Heidegger to an already heavy course load in philosophy. And yet there still remained in him a wild restlessness that at times seemed almost out of control.

He had also begun to display a sharply critical attitude toward others that at times bordered on cruelty. He was headstrong in his opinions. His general unpleasantness cost him friendships and made his confreres wary of him. When his harsh behavior was pointed out to him, he apologized humbly, as docile as a child, but it was usually not long before he repeated the behavior. There were times during these years when superiors raised the question of dismissing him from the Society of Jesus because of his inability to fit in.

A story circulated in later years that, together with another scholastic, Delp somehow obtained pharmaceutical stimulants and, on at least one occasion—disregarding the strict rule of silence and lights out after nine o'clock—stayed up all night to study. If true, such activity could only have exacerbated a psychological imbalance that was already in evidence.

In 1931, when his philosophy studies came to an end, Delp moved on to the next phase of his Jesuit life, the so-called regency period of apostolic work. For this work, he was sent back to Feldkirch in Austria, to the large boys' boarding school called Stella Matutina, which had been established in 1856. The school was a sprawling complex, built along both sides of the Ill River. Housing nearly five hundred boys, the school itself was almost a small village. Students from all over Europe attended Stella Matutina; from the time of its founding, European Catholic nobility had sent their sons there. The boys were grouped according to age, with two scholastics, called prefects, in charge of each group. Delp was assigned as a prefect to group five, which was composed of eighty-seven boys between seventeen and nineteen years of age. The prefects slept in curtained cubicles in the same dormitories as the boys, with just enough room for a bed and a washstand. Here, Delp found an outlet for his prodigious energy and also discovered a talent for working with young people.

In addition to his attempts at teaching the boys according to the Jesuit style of education—arguing their positions and supporting their arguments with logical, objective reasons—Delp also introduced a Neudeutschland style of allegiance to a Christian way of life: flag-waving, field games, and a marching song: "Wave the banner. . . . Christ, Lord of the new time!" The idea was to replace the staid old style of deportment and behavior (up to now, the students' main means of exercise had been going for walks) with an entirely new spirit. Delp also adopted a partnership style of teaching that appealed to the students. One of his accomplishments was a series of plays performed during Advent one year, the central theme of which he described thus: "Christmas means that God touches us, that he takes our hands and places them on his heart, that God comes to us and makes us free. That says it all; Christmas is nothing other than that God is with us."[3]

Photographs of Delp during his three years at Stella Matutina show him lounging with his charges, hardly distinguishable from them except for his clerical clothes. In one photo, the boys sit on either side of him, relaxed and dressed in ties and breeches. Everyone is grinning at the camera, and Delp is leaning back with his shoulders slightly hunched. Smoke rises from the cigarette in his hand, his legs are crossed, and his long cassock is slightly hitched up. It is one of the few photos from the early part of his life in which he actually looks happy.

This was also the sort of pose that seemed calculated to provoke his immediate superior, the man with whom he was to be connected in a crucial way for the rest of his life: the head prefect, Augustin Rösch. Fourteen years older than Delp, Rösch was of a different generation. He had served as a soldier in World War I and had been wounded several times, winning medals for distinguished bravery and service. He was also a Jesuit of the old school, trained in a milieu of simple piety and unblinking obedience. Though known to be kind and fatherly to those in his charge, he was also a man of steely discipline as a result of the military formation he had received both in the army and in the Society of Jesus.

During Delp's tenure at Stella Matutina, Rösch became the school's rector. Rösch was certainly aware of the young man's intellectual ability, but he ran into difficulties with Delp's personality, and the two men's teaching methods clashed. He disapproved of the Neudeutschland rallying style that Delp introduced to the distinguished school. He seems as well to have been displeased with Delp's influence over the boys, but it is unclear whether his disapproval stemmed from personal jealousy or a desire to rein in the scholastic's strong rebellious streak and mold him according to his

Delp with an unidentified companion at Pullach, around 1930. *Courtesy of the Archives of the Upper German Province of the Society of Jesus (Archivum Monacense SJ), Munich.*

own model of obedience. Or, yet again, Rösch may have been subject to the helpless realization that here was a member of the new wave of Jesuits, an original, someone who could not be tamed in the manner of the old rules.

These were tense years for the German contingent at Stella Matutina as they watched political events unfold across the Austrian border. The Jesuits cannot have rejoiced when Hitler was named chancellor of Germany on January 30, 1933, or when he called a snap election at the beginning of March, putting himself firmly in power, or when the moderate Catholic Center Party capitulated to the new regime. Apart from everything else on the Nazi agenda, it was clear from the beginning that, as Judge Roland Freisler was to say years later at Delp's trial, National Socialism and Christianity had only one thing in common: they both demanded the allegiance

Augustin Rösch. *Courtesy of the Archives of the Upper German Province of the Society of Jesus (Archivum Monacense SJ), Munich.*

of the whole person.[4] Yet the Nazis now formed Germany's duly elected government. The implicit attitude of the German Catholic hierarchy pointed to the importance of patriotic acceptance of legitimate authority. The bishops did not want another Kulturkampf waged against the Church. And so on May 1, 1933, an annual day of pilgrimage to a nearby shrine, the German youths at Stella Matutina gathered around a radio and heard Joseph Goebbels, the new minister for propaganda, make a special appeal to German youth. Then they stood and cheered and sang the German national anthem before joining the others on the pilgrimage.

Not long afterward, however, the Nazi strong-arm authority came down directly on Stella Matutina in the form of a decree that a thousand reichsmark were to be paid to the German government for every German citizen living outside the country. The result was a decision to shut down the German part of the school and reestablish it in Germany. On the day they took leave in March 1934, the German boys marched away from the school in long rows, with Delp alongside dressed in his black cassock. The boys sang as they headed through the town to the railroad station in Feldkirch, where they boarded a train for the Black Forest. There, the Jesuits set up a school at St. Blasien, in a facility that had once been a Benedictine monastery.

By this time Germany had become a totalitarian state: all non-Nazi political parties and trade unions had been destroyed, and indeed, all organizations, even nonpolitical ones, were forced to either become Nazi organizations or suffer harassment and ultimately dissolution. In the face of this rapid development, the Vatican had negotiated a concordat with the Nazi regime that was intended to safeguard the rights of the Catholic Church. Included in the concordat was the guarantee that Catholic schools could continue to function on the condition that instruction remain strictly in the religious sphere.

At St. Blasien, however, as in all the schools throughout Germany, the Hitler Youth made speedy inroads with propaganda campaigns to attract idealistic and patriotic youth. Trying to appease the authorities became a tightrope act for the Jesuits. Although the marching, flag-waving style of the Hitler Youth was similar to that of the Catholic youth groups, no common ground existed with an ideology that was antithetical to Christianity. Even their methods of attracting youth differed: the Hitler Youth relied on feverish, emotional discipleship rather than reasoned argument, on disorder and aggression rather than discipline. Nazi excitement was building among the students, however, and Delp's reaction was to try injecting Christian principles into their enthusiasm. The effort resulted in deep unease. Many years later, a student remembered that Delp still laughed loudly and easily with them, but when he supervised study periods, he looked deep in thought as he took long strides up and down the rows, arms folded, chin thrust out, staring into space. This particular posture earned him the nickname "Bullus," after an English motorcycle racer of the day named Thomas F. Bullus, who struck the same pose. Delp was to later use this nickname as one of his pseudonyms in his prison letters.

In the years ahead, the Jesuit schools were to close one by one, some of them directly by the Nazis and others by the Jesuits themselves because of the intolerable conditions imposed on them.

Theology Studies

In April 1934, shortly after his arrival at St. Blasien, Delp left for Ignatiuskolleg in Valkenburg, Netherlands, to begin his theology studies. Ignatiuskolleg was yet another German Jesuit institution that had been established outside of Germany during Bismarck's Kulturkampf. It stood along the edge of a forest not far across the border from the city of Aachen, among hills known as the "Alps of Holland." The enormous college had more than 350 rooms, a chapel with thirty-one side altars in addition to the main altar, and a library with more than two hundred thousand books, the largest private collection of books in Holland.

At Ignatiuskolleg, food was scarce and the diet dull ("applesauce is varied by introducing pear sauce," wrote an American scholastic in a letter home in the mid-1930s).[5] Because of its peculiar situation—an institution operating with German funds outside Germany—Ignatiuskolleg found itself in a financial bind when the Nazi government passed a law that prohibited sending money out of the country. The Jesuit magazine *America* reported the situation: "Dispatches from the Hague blamed the German money laws for financial troubles from which the German Jesuit seminary at Valkenburg, Dutch Limburg, is suffering. Because of the German 'blockade' the seminary is deprived of normal financial relations with Germany and so finds great difficulty not only in maintaining its library and scientific departments and paying taxes to the Dutch Government but even in supplying the necessities of its 250 students."[6] The report went on to say that Dutch Catholics were coming to the Jesuits' aid through food drives and special Sunday collections.

Despite the hardships and his cautionary brush with the Nazi system at St. Blasien, Delp jumped into his studies with his usual enthusiasm. Five classes each day took place—in fundamental theology, Church history, patristics, Scripture study, and moral and pastoral theology. Practicums to prepare the scholastics for their work as priests sometimes involved confessional role-play in which the professor played the penitent, spilling out hair-raising confessions. Normally there was only a half-hour of recreation each day.

A cosmopolitan energy hummed throughout the student body, with scholastics attending from all over Europe as well as the United States. (The Spaniard Pedro Arrupe, who would later become the Jesuit superior-general, was also a student there at the time.) The scholastics roamed the forest trails on their free days, and each morning they walked the college's large, wooded garden, praying their rosaries privately or stopping by the shrines that dotted the pathways. The songbirds, the woodland animals, and the freshness of the early morning mist provided a relief from their heavy academic load and from their awareness of the fury that was building just a few short miles away across the German border.

Stories regularly reached Valkenburg of the upheavals taking place in Germany: the Nuremberg Laws legitimized the harassment of Jews; many Catholic organizations were dissolved and the Catholic youth movements were outlawed, a direct violation of the 1933 concordat with the Vatican. Priests throughout Germany were monitored for anti-Nazi sentiments in their preaching. Those whose sermons were considered dangerous to the regime were taken into custody.

Jesuits were already suspect. A family's standard was lowered in the eyes of the Nazis when a son entered the Society of Jesus, and eventually it became illegal for the Jesuits to accept any new candidates at all. One Jesuit had been jailed for a year for calling Christ "Führer" in spite of being acquitted of any wrongdoing. Two other Jesuits were arrested and jailed for preaching against the theories of Alfred Rosenberg, whose writings formed the basis of Nazi ideology. The new arbitrariness of law—that arguing on the basis of fact no longer mattered—caused disquiet. There were stories of Jesuits taken into custody and interrogated for hours without recourse to legal help; one of them quoted his interrogator: "I know the Jesuits and their mental reservations."[7] News arrived of an inspection at St. Blasien; when the rector requested the Nazi inspectors' credentials, they simply brushed past him and entered the building on their own authority. The German economy was improving, but only because of the burgeoning numbers of munitions factories all over the country. By the end of 1936, there was open talk that Europe was preparing for war.

None of these developments were lost on Delp, who, like other German scholastics, realized that the Nazis had already begun to wage war on their own citizens, and that he was soon to be heading into the fire. With some of his fellow Jesuits, he wrote *The Rebuilding,* a book that discussed the kind of society that should come into being once National Socialism had been stamped out. Delp was as hotheaded as ever, but he was also seen as open-minded, eager for new ideas, and always in tune with the latest thinking. He also discovered a new talent: preaching, which would become a vehicle for allowing others to share in his own deepening prayer life.

While he was in Valkenburg, Delp's work on the philosophy of Martin Heidegger, *Tragische Existenz* (Tragic Existence), was published. A sense of spiritual dislocation in the wake of World War I had provided the ground for Heidegger's thinking, which sought to explore the relationship between philosophy and contemporary life. Heidegger's attempts struck a chord with Delp, who liked Heidegger's stand on the place of humanity: the human person is the master of matter, not its slave. Delp rejected Heidegger's final conclusion, however, because it dealt only with finite humanity and therefore placed huge limitations on the human person. In the end, Delp believed that Heidegger's philosophy was a call to "tragic existence," an existence that ultimately led to meaninglessness and hopelessness. It seemed to propose a theology in which God did not exist. In later years, Karl Rahner and others criticized Delp's work for its misunderstanding of the philosophical foundation of Heidegger's work and its dated, moralistic tone.

But Delp's study of Heidegger did lay the groundwork for his own thinking—that humanity without God is not humanity at all—and it provided the opportunity for him to develop what would become a major theme in his own writing. He saw humanity as moving in a dynamism of opposites, and he sought a way to bring the opposites together into a creative synthesis, what he called the "missing center." He interpreted Germany's historical distress in these terms—danger leading to protest and reaction, which in turn became a new source of danger—and, as his thinking progressed during the next few years, his life's work gradually became clear to him: helping his country discover its missing center. His study of Heidegger heightened his alertness and his desire to unmask falsehoods.

In October 1936, Delp left Valkenburg for the seminary of St. Georg in Frankfurt to finish his theological studies and make his immediate preparation for ordination to the priesthood. In April 1937, in a burst of filial fervor after his ordination as a deacon, he wrote to Augustin Rösch, who two years earlier had been named the provincial superior of the Upper German Jesuit province: "This is truly a beautiful time, and I have had only vigorous and happy days since becoming a Catholic and since entering the Society of Jesus eleven years ago. Someone sent me an ordination card with the text, 'Your youth will be renewed. . . .' That is really the way it is."[8]

CHAPTER 3

WAR AND
PRIESTLY MINISTRY

1937–1941

On June 24, 1937, Delp was ordained a priest beneath the high dome and gold baroque backdrop of the high altar of St. Michael's Church in Munich. On July 4 he celebrated his first solemn High Mass in his hometown church of St. Andreas in Lampertheim. After the ceremony, the Delp family posed for photographs with the new priest. The choir sang the Te Deum, and in the afternoon the parish held a reception and Solemn Vespers. The celebration continued the following day, when Delp officiated at the wedding of his sister Greta to Fritz Kern. Few such happy days remained for Delp in the company of his family.

He returned to Frankfurt in the fall to complete his studies, and in July 1938 he received his licentiate in theology. The following September he left for Starnberger See, south of Munich, to spend his tertianship, the Jesuit's final year of formation before formal entry into the ministry of the Church. He was thirty-one years old, with a heaviness around his jaws and neck that gave him the look of early middle age. The seriousness that marked his face still dissipated when he smiled, however; his robust energy remained, and

Delp with his family on the occasion of his first Solemn High Mass, July 4, 1937. Front row, from left: Gerda (Delp) Florschütz, Lucia Florschütz, Friedrich Delp, Maria Delp, Greta (Delp) Kern. Back row, from left: Philipp Florschütz, Maia (Brückmann) Delp, Ewald Delp, Alfred Delp, Fritz Kern, Fritz Delp. *Courtesy of Marianne Junk.*

his restlessness was now channeled into the new challenges that faced him.

To be a Jesuit priest in Germany in the late 1930s was no inconsequential matter. In March 1937, Pope Pius XI had issued the encyclical *Mit brennender Sorge* (With Burning Concern) on the Church and the German Reich, which decried the abrogation of civil rights and the suffering of innocent people, especially the deliberate infliction of hardship based on race. The encyclical, written in German rather than the usual Latin, was clandestinely printed in Germany and hand-delivered to Catholic churches throughout the country on the night of March 13. It was read from the pulpits the following day, Passion Sunday, before the Nazis even knew of its existence. The document was written in the careful, turgid language of Vatican diplomacy, and, as a result, its central message may have been lost on many listeners in the pews; nevertheless, the encyclical caused a furor among the Nazi leadership. By the end of the day, nearly all copies had been confiscated, and the twelve companies that had printed the document were immediately closed down. Partly in retaliation for this subterfuge, the Nazis began to plan a campaign against all the Christian churches, determining to infiltrate their systems at every level. Within the Catholic Church, the Jesuits were considered particularly dangerous.

The Nazis had good reasons for distrusting the Jesuits. As a group, Jesuits were very well educated and highly regarded as educators of youth. They were well connected (Jesuits had been consulted in the drafting of the concordat; and a German Jesuit, Robert Leiber, who worked closely with Cardinal Eugenio Pacelli, the Vatican Secretary of State, was to become his assistant when Pacelli became Pope Pius XII), and they had a history of strong loyalty to the Church. Although Jesuit reaction to Nazism was not as uniform as the Nazis thought (a few Jesuits were slow to recognize its incompatibility with Christianity, and at least one was known to argue that Hitler had been misunderstood), the monthly Jesuit publication *Stimmen der Zeit* had been openly critical of the regime as early as 1933.

A campaign of harassment against the Society of Jesus had been underway for a number of years. Defamatory articles about the Jesuits were published regularly in the daily newspapers. A cartoon, typical of the propaganda campaign, showed a Nazi pulling across a curtain to reveal a Freemason, a Jew, and a Jesuit scheming together around a table. *Stimmen der Zeit* was forced to cease publication from December 1935 to March 1936. In 1935, the Munich police had issued a confidential report, "Safeguarding Against the Jesuits," on how public statements by Jesuits were to be handled. The statement read, "These lectures . . . are so ambiguously and cunningly composed that a juridical punishment of the lecturer is possible in only very few cases." The report insisted it was especially important that Jesuits be carefully watched in Catholic Bavaria and that any Jesuits speaking against the state be punished with "protective custody." The report also ordered that "public appearances of the Jesuits are to be reported immediately, and even if no activities are observed, a report is to be made on the 30th of every month starting from May 30, 1935."[1] The Jesuit schools and residences throughout Germany continued to be raided. The aim of the harassment campaign against the Jesuits and other clergy was to portray them as criminal suspects so as not to arouse sympathy for them among the general population.

In Munich, the Nazis continually came head to head with the Jesuit who had become the provincial superior of the Upper German province in 1935, Augustin Rösch, Delp's former rector at Stella Matutina. In Rösch, the Nazis met their match. Still in his forties, Rösch combined maturity and experience with a youthful energy. He had been schooled as a fierce defender of the Catholic Church and had immediately been aware, when the Nazis came into power, that they intended to rid the country of Christianity. Moreover, Rösch was a World War I hero, a distinction that he enjoyed throwing in the face of the Gestapo during his frequent confrontations with them. He encouraged defiance during the many raids on Jesuit houses and schools. Some years later, Rösch recalled that when the cardinal archbishop of Munich suggested that he give in and have the Jesuits leave one of the houses voluntarily, he refused. It was a matter of principle, he insisted; the confiscation of property was illegal, and, once begun, the practice would continue right across the country.

In spring 1938, however, there was no option for Stella Matutina, where Rösch had spent years educating boys and where he and Delp had locked horns: the Nazis annexed Austria, and the proud Jesuit school that had educated generations of Catholic leaders was forced to close its doors.

The Nazis also singled out individual Jesuits. Oswald von Nell-Breuning, who was responsible for much of *Quadragesimo Anno,* was harassed. Friedrich Muckermann, the editor of the Catholic publication *Der Gral,* ran into trouble with the Nazis; he fled to Switzerland in 1934 and was tried in absentia for high treason. Several other Jesuits throughout Germany were removed from their posts because of their preaching. The popular Mario von Galli was said to have warned the Nazi spies in his Stuttgart congregation to pay close attention to particular points in his sermons. Later, when von Galli was told by a Nazi official that he would be banished to Switzerland for life, he allegedly gave the cocky reply, "Whose life?" [2]

And then there was the most dangerous Jesuit of all as far as the Nazis were concerned, and the closest to Delp: Rupert Mayer. Mayer had been an army chaplain and had lost a leg helping injured soldiers during World War I. He had taken a stand against Nazism as early as 1923, when in a debate he had argued against the question, Can Catholics be National Socialists? In the intervening years, he had became a powerful and hugely popular preacher. From the splendid blue-gray pulpit of Munich's St. Michael's Church, Mayer preached against the Nazis and always drew large crowds.

In late spring 1937, shortly before Delp's ordination, Mayer was arrested. Six weeks later, he was sentenced to six months in prison on the grounds of "improper use of the pulpit." Mayer would be released and rearrested a number of times in the following years; he was finally placed under house arrest in a Benedictine monastery until the end of the war. Delp, who lived in the same residence as Mayer for a short time before his ordination and whose fledgling sermons were delivered in the same pulpit from

Rupert Mayer. *Courtesy of the Archives of the Upper German Province of the Society of Jesus (Archivum Monacense SJ), Munich.*

which fearless preaching had sent Mayer to prison, could not have been unaffected by Mayer's courage.

The tertianship, however, in the rural tranquility of Starnberger See, provided a period of intense personal prayer for Delp. He made jottings in his journal that reflected the path he wanted to take: "[God] must play a greater role in my life than before. I must live personally with God." "Move away from myself. Learn service and sacrifice. I've been a big egoist."[3] He also wrote about the theme of the Sacred Heart, which he regarded not as simple piety but as the very center of the Christian life and which was to play a significant role at the end of his life: "The heart of Jesus as the symbol of God's nearness to humanity." "Heart of Jesus, doorway to the Trinity."[4]

Nazi violence, however, was never far away from the pastoral, introspective life. Kristallnacht, the night of savage attacks against

Jews all over Germany, took place in November of 1938. By Christmas, the Jesuit tertians were forced to move because of threats to expropriate some of the Jesuit institutions.

In late spring 1939, Delp received permission from his superiors to begin his doctoral studies in philosophy. His application to the University of Munich was turned down with the written statement, "Permission for the member of the Jesuit Order Alfred Delp for studies in philosophy or in any other academic faculty cannot be granted."[5] An alternate plan, to become an army chaplain, was also turned down. And so in July Delp went to Munich, not to study, but to take up writing and editorial duties at *Stimmen der Zeit*. The publication's office was located on Veterinärstrasse, in a four-story building that also housed the twelve Jesuits who worked there.

The small street formed a pleasant link between the University of Munich and the huge park and series of landscaped gardens known as *Englischer Garten*. To the right of the building was a tall fountain in front of the university, and to the left, the park's thick trees, which could be mistaken for a rural woodland. It was perhaps possible, during the few tense weeks that remained in the summer of 1939, for Delp to lose himself in the *Englischer Garten* amid the late-blooming flowers, and watch the gentle flow of the Isar River.

At another time, the nearness to the university's intellectual life would have excited him, but the university had now rejected him, and he had to rely on the intellectual atmosphere provided by his fellow Jesuits and on his own quiet and contemplative thought. His manner, both personal and intellectual, continued to be confrontational. He still loved to debate and to bore into the hearts of questions and theories.

Up to now, Delp had spent only brief periods of time in Munich, a city of many parks and flowering gardens. Munich's days of imperial grandeur as the jewel of Bavaria were now gone. It had become the spiritual and cultural center of National Socialism. Hitler had claimed Munich as his home base since World War I, and his plan was to make the whole city a monument to Nazism. Public buildings, constructed with expansive façades and heavy concrete pillars, were planned to overshadow the city's Renaissance architecture. In the new art gallery—built to house neoclassical, Nazi-approved statues and paintings—collections of modern abstract art were denounced as degenerate and destroyed. At the Odeonsplatz, a military monument became a shrine commemorating sixteen Nazis who had been killed there during the skirmish that sixteen years earlier had made Hitler decide to turn his bullying tactics into politically acceptable ones. Huge red banners with the swastika at the center hung down between the monument's pillars. People were now required to give the Nazi salute as they passed by (a mandate that some were already avoiding by finding alternate routes). State police, now called the Gestapo, and military men in jackboots swarmed the streets and often marched wave upon wave in perfect columns with banners and flags, singing in powerful unison to pounding drums while crowds cheered and chanted the now-common German greeting, "Heil Hitler!"

Other sights also greeted Delp as he walked the city streets: huge piles of rubble where synagogues once stood, the vacant fronts of Jewish businesses with broken windows that revealed debris-strewn interiors, people scurrying about with fearful and furtive looks. And there were disquieting rumors: a campaign of murder was said to have begun against mentally ill patients. (Two Jesuits, institutionalized because of mental illness, were to die in this way.) For several years, concentration camps had been going up all over the country; one had been built in nearby Dachau. Anyone who had differences with the regime was threatened with Dachau, and some had already been sent—notably Communists and Socialists—under the euphemistic phrase, "protective custody," without recourse to the usual legal channels.

Almost a year earlier, Hitler had signed an agreement with Britain and France in one of the new Nazi buildings known as the Führerbau. It was to become known as the Munich Agreement and would shortly prove meaningless. Hitler had already moved in on Czechoslovakia, and German troops were poised to invade Poland. As Alfred Delp, after thirteen years of preparation, finally embarked on his priestly ministry, his country was setting the stage for war.

On September 1, 1939, German tanks stormed across Poland, and the war began. When the German army defeated the Polish troops a few weeks later, Nazi propaganda began in earnest. For the first few years of the war, it seemed as if the Nazi boasts would be fulfilled. By June 1940, there was victory upon victory as the countries of Western Europe fell one by one—Holland, then Belgium, then France. In the summer of 1941, the German offensive began along the eastern front in a bid to conquer Russia. Within six months, the tide began slowly to turn. By then, thousands of German soldiers had fallen in the bitter Russian campaign. Among them was Delp's brother-in-law Fritz Kern, whose wife, Greta, was left with a three-year-old daughter, Marianne.

Throughout the flag-flying victories and into the period when defeat seemed probable and he became aware of the atrocities committed in the name of the German people, Delp continued to develop some of the ideas he had been thinking about for the previous few years. He had become the resident expert on the "social question," especially as outlined in *Quadragesimo Anno*. He continued to work on theories to counteract the Nazi teaching of "mass man" with its doctrinaire belief in the primacy of the state over the rights of the individual. He was less interested in politics as such than in the idea of the nation and in the nation's duty to reflect the dignity and authority of God in its relationship to its citizens. Religion, he concluded, was necessary as the nation's foundation stone, and the process of secularization, making human beings nonreligious, remained for him a fundamental problem.

A further problem existed, in his view, in the Church's blindness to this calamity. "Has the Church forgotten 'Thou shalt not'? Has the Church forgotten the commandments, or is she keeping quiet because she is convinced that her clear and firm preaching is hopeless?" he asked rhetorically at a diocesan conference in Fulda in 1941.[6] His interest in political thinking and his Protestant formation as a youth had given him a breadth of vision that moved beyond the boundaries of Catholicism, and he regarded the Church as too parochial and inward-looking. To his way of thinking, the matter of fundamental human rights was a religious concern, and he deplored the extreme caution that led to the Church's inclination toward silence in the face of the state's disregard for these rights.

From 1940 onward, Delp became involved in the "Mission to Men" conferences. Established in the wake of the Nazi battle against Catholicism, these conferences aimed to give spiritual sustenance to Catholic men in order to keep them rooted and strong in their faith. This was a further opportunity for Delp to develop his thoughts, and he became known for his enthusiastic, powerful preaching. He was subtle and clever in naming the crimes of the regime without getting himself into trouble. In November 1941, for example, after viewing the Nazi propaganda film on euthanasia *Ich klage an! (I Accuse!)*, he preached on the film's ideas. It represented, he said, "an escape from the difficulty of love and community," adding that "even if all a person's organs are gone and he can no longer express himself as a human being, he still is human and there still remains a constant call toward an inner nobility and a call to love and sacrificial strength for those who live around him. If you deprive people of the ability to nurse and heal their sick, you make human beings into egotistical predators who are interested only in their own pleasant life."[7]

Some days afterward, he presented St. Elizabeth of Hungary (who had lived most of her life in Germany and was one of the country's patron saints) as an exemplar of human life: "This quiet woman bears a grave and urgent message for our land, for our people, for each of us. Everywhere, wherever we find ourselves, wherever we may be called upon to bear witness, we must protect life, we must guard human beings from everything that can crush them underfoot. Woe to those who inflict suffering! And woe to those who have destroyed a human life, who have desecrated an image of God, even when it was already breathing its last, even when it seemed to represent only a vestige of humanity."[8]

His talks often broached the theme that he later developed into what he called the Third Idea.[9] He perceived human beings of the West as caught between two opposing extreme worldviews: one view of the person as individualistic, self-sufficient, and materialistic, and the other of collectivist Bolshevism, in which human beings were treated as mere functionaries. As he saw it, most people thrashed their way between these two extremes. The Third Idea was an attempt to develop the theory of a new social order to supersede both capitalism and Communism. It was necessary, he wrote, that a person's rights to life, freedom, and property be connected to the restructuring of economic systems along socialist lines. Relationships between employers and employees should be spelled out, and he regarded the papal social encyclicals as the foundation stone of such relations.

During this period, Delp wrote a small book called *Humanity and History*. This work developed a related interest, the tension between the eternal and the temporal, history and the present moment. The point of intersection is always the human being at any given moment, he wrote, and the human being's responsibility is always to reflect the image of God. And finally, it is God as revealed by Jesus Christ who is the ultimate nexus of the present moment and the eternal. As the society in which he lived sank further into depravity, he saw no other hope for humanity than placing God at the center of that society.

In December 1940, the Nazis began an effort to mow down the Catholic religious communities of Germany by closing their houses. Earlier in the year, they had considered expelling all Jesuits from Germany and Austria and then rejected the plan. In Germany, such an action would have been too visible and blatant a violation of the concordat, they decided, and in Austria there was fear that expulsion of the Jesuits would give the large Catholic population reason to turn en masse against the Reich. The previous July, when the Jesuit college in Pullach had been turned into an army hospital, the Jesuit community had been allowed to remain. But now a systematic swath-cutting of all Catholic religious orders took place in earnest. The first action happened in Fulda, where a Franciscan monastery was ransacked and then closed and the community scattered. Four months later, at twenty minutes to three on April 18, 1941, eight Gestapo officers came to the door of *Stimmen der Zeit* with the statement that "for the protection of the people and the state" the publication was to cease operation and the building was to be confiscated. The inhabitants had two hours' notice to vacate. The closing of *Stimmen der Zeit* was not a surprise: by this time, the Nazis had closed down and dissolved nearly all the Catholic publications and organizations.

St. Georg's Church

Stimmen der Zeit's Jesuit staff scattered to find accommodation else-where. Delp was named rector of the church of St. Georg in the well-to-do suburb of Bogenhausen. The church was a small baroque building surrounded by a high brick wall. Just outside the wall sat the parish house, originally a farmhouse, where Delp made his residence. The house served as a diocesan service center from which other priests and four Vincentian sisters conducted their work as well.

It was the perfect assignment for the displaced Jesuit. St. Georg's had been integrated into the larger Precious Blood parish, and so Delp was not responsible for any pastoral duties other than cele-brating the Mass and other sacraments. He was free to continue his study and writing as well as participate in the conferences that by now took him to various dioceses throughout the country and as far away as Vienna.

At St. Georg's, for the first time in his life as a Jesuit Delp was in close contact with families and the common concerns of everyday life. His former delight in working with youth was also renewed; although youth groups were no longer allowed unless they were asso-ciated with the Hitler Youth, he organized them anyway and gave religion lessons to the young people, instructing them to leave their bicycles on the street away from the church so as not to attract atten-tion. Delp wrote to a friend, "The parents of Bogenhausen's flag-waving youth can be reassured. My youth are in good order (note the emphasis on *my*)."[10] He belted out songs and hymns with abandon (his favorite: "Let Us Sing a Song of Joy") in his tone-deaf manner and took groups of young people on weekend camping trips.

Shortly after he arrived at St. Georg's, a notice came down that religious articles were to be removed from Catholic schools. Along with other priests, especially throughout Bavaria, Delp jumped into the fray: groups of teachers and parents chose the subversive

Delp sailing on the Simsee, around 1943. *Courtesy of the Archives of the Upper German Province of the Society of Jesus (Archivum Monacense SJ), Munich.*

route of removing statues and religious pictures as they were told and then replacing them with crucifixes that had been blessed by the priests. For a short time after the summer of 1941, Delp also became known as "an address" for fleeing Jews on the underground route to the safety of Switzerland.

He poured his enormous energy into all these activities. He now wore secular clothes—suit and tie—which gave him an over-all owlish and rumpled look. He smoked heavily, and a new friend, Karl Kreuser, supplied him with cigars. Clouds of smoke and a pervasive cigar smell surrounded him. He was becoming well known for the calm, contemplative quality of his sermons, which were often taken down in shorthand, reproduced, and handed from person to person on paper folded down to the size of a thimble to escape detection. A seriousness had settled over him, but the discussion groups he organized brought vibrancy to his voice, and when he relaxed his manner grew animated. With maturity and the gravity of life around him, his overbearing manner had melted to some extent into a pleasant and attractive vitality.

At St. Georg's, Delp also became a spiritual guide. One person recalled that he often gave her the sequence prayer "Come Holy Spirit" from the Pentecost Mass as a penance after confession. When she asked him why he seemed intent on this particular penance, he replied that he couldn't think of a more beautiful prayer. He spoke often of Peter, a favorite Gospel figure of his, seeing in this apostle a combination of impetuousness, frailty, and passionate trust—qualities that defined Delp himself.

In the spring of 1941, he was invited by his artist friend Ruth Flamm to spend his vacation at a small hamlet southeast of Munich called Wolferkam, which was a cluster of farmhouses owned by various members of one family near a lake known as Simssee. He had a room in one of the farmhouses and took part in the family's activities, enjoying the rhythms of country life: swimming, sailing, mountain climbing, helping in the fields. He said Mass and preached in the small, nearby church. The family environment—with sounds of children's laughter and quarreling, the kitchen smells, the good-natured bantering—brought an element of family earthiness to his life. It was a contrast to the Nazi harshness that greeted him at every turn in Munich. He also made friends with artists in the area with whom he could discuss his thoughts and sound out his ideas.

He was at his happiest in this tranquil setting, calling it "The Isle of Happiness," and he returned the following two summers, bringing with him his widowed sister, Greta, and her daughter, Marianne. He had assumed a fatherly interest in his young niece. During this vacation time, he took on a parental role, taking her to look at the farm animals, and, at mealtime, insisting she eat everything on her plate.

Greta Kern and her daughter, Marianne. *Courtesy of Marianne Junk.*

After returning to Munich one year, he wrote back to Wolferkam complaining of a "vacation hangover." He explained further: "One gets a normal hangover when one drinks too much in the evening and then wakes up in the morning and has to go to work seeing everything through a blue haze. One gets a vacation hangover when everything has gone well for too long, when one has been spoiled and pampered, when one has done nothing, when one has been sur-rounded only by good people and good weather, open land, the lake, the wind, the sun and tall trees, all of it at one's fingertips; and suddenly, the opposite happens. Suddenly one is back in the city and at work, with people who all want something, and often that's not all. Unpleasant people too are always around."[11]

It is possible that the Gestapo was already nosing about, perhaps watching him and listening to his sermons. It was already known that when a church minister suspected by the Gestapo was preach-ing, one or two unfamiliar men might be seen sitting in the back, intent on the speaker, quietly taking notes.

THE "FRIENDS" OF THE KREISAU CIRCLE

1941–1943

The Jesuits were by now perennial suspects, and none more so than the provincial superior of the Upper German province and Delp's old adversary, Augustin Rösch. Toward the end of 1940, in an all-out bid to rid Germany of Jesuits, the Gestapo had set up a file with the names of all German Jesuits, and the following year, Hitler gave a personal order to have Jesuits declared unfit for war service and expelled from the armed forces. (For several reasons, this order was ignored in some parts of the army, and a number of Jesuits remained in the military—priests and brothers as chaplains and medical aides, and scholastics as soldiers.) The *gauleiter*, or district political leader, of Munich predicted that soon all the Jesuits in Germany would be transported to the concentration camps in the East. Rösch was trailed by the Gestapo, questioned, and threatened with incarceration at Dachau.

But the Jesuit superior had hit his stride in his outspoken opposition to Nazi persecution of the Catholic Church. As the noose tightened around other areas of Catholicism, Rösch acted as a liaison among the bishops, and through his Jesuit contacts in Rome, he also established a link with the Vatican. A sharp mind and considerable negotiating skills made him excel at the job. He even seemed to relish it at times, trying out various disguises in his effort to get around the country. In the later war years, when it became difficult for civilians to use trains, he managed to get space for himself by pretending to be a railway worker.

According to an account Rösch gave after the war, he was walking on a street in Berlin one day in October 1941, when he heard Hitler's raucous voice blaring from overhead loudspeakers, trumpeting an imminent victory in Russia. He felt overwhelmed with despondency over an apparently unlimited Nazi triumph. Just then, a friend from Bavaria approached him, an aristocrat by the name of Baron Karl Ludwig von Guttenberg. "Why so serious, Father?" the baron asked.

Rösch told him about his sense of discouragement in the face of Nazi progress, and Guttenberg, indicating that the conversation would be better held elsewhere, whispered that he knew someone whom Rösch should meet. He told the Jesuit to walk behind him, leaving some distance between them. "When I stop at a garden gate to light a cigarette, you enter at the next garden gate, go around a large garage, and up a staircase at the back. An apartment is up there. Knock on the door and give my name as the password."[1]

Rösch did as he was instructed and knocked at the door of the flat. The door was opened by a very lean man, well over six feet tall, with slightly stooped shoulders and a receding hairline that emphasized his long serious face and quiet gaze. This man was thirty-four-year-old Count Helmuth James von Moltke.

Rösch, like anyone familiar with German history, knew the Moltke name. The count's great-great-uncle, Helmuth von Moltke,

Helmuth James von Moltke with
his son Caspar. *Courtesy of Freya
von Moltke.*

had been a Prussian military hero. Because his mother was South
African of Scottish descent, the young Helmuth James had come to
adulthood with not only near-perfect fluency in English, but also a
wide-ranging view of the world. He had a quietly cheerful disposi-
tion, a wry sense of humor, and a serious cast to his personality that
made him seem older than his years. As a twenty-two-year-old law
student, the young aristocrat had managed his family's estate in
Kreisau, Silesia, and then had completed his law studies with a special interest in politics and economics. He had a deep mistrust of the
flag-waving brand of nationalism that had gathered steam after
World War I, and because he believed in democracy, he supported
the Weimar Republic. He noted with alarm the rise of Nazi popu-
larity and established an office in Berlin specializing in international
law while keeping a foot in the democratic world through contacts

with such bodies as the League of Nations and the International Court at the Hague. Along the way, he looked after the affairs of Jews and other German citizens who were fleeing the country. When the war broke out in 1939, he took a job with the Abwehr, the intelligence division of the German armed forces.

As the war progressed through the first few months, Moltke became convinced that the Nazi victory could not possibly last, and an idea began to unfold: start now to plan for the rebuilding of Germany after that inevitable end; establish a new constitution that will never again allow a totalitarian dictatorship to develop. As he saw it, society needed a rebirth, with small communities in which people could participate rather than be alienated. He also began to see a need for a transnational authority because he believed the overly nationalistic sense that had been displayed in Germany would ultimately destroy humanity.

Aware of his relative inexperience, he sought out people who thought along similar lines, with expertise in industry, economics, and politics. Moltke's first contact was Peter Yorck von Wartenburg, a fellow aristocrat and lawyer. Others were gradually approached: Julius Leber, a socialist and intellectual with close ties to labor unions; Adam von Trott, a Rhodes scholar with many English contacts; and Hans-Bernd von Haeften, who along with Trott provided important links with the foreign office. Haeften, a Lutheran whose opposition to Nazism sprang from religious convictions, brought to the group a strong commitment to Christian principles, and soon the Lutheran pastors Eugen Gerstenmaier and Harald Poelchau were invited to the group's discussions. Gerstenmaier was a theologian and intellectual; Poelchau, the Protestant chaplain at the Tegel Prison in Berlin, had been a student of the theologian Paul Tillich. Some prominent members of the by-now-defunct Catholic Center Party—men such as Hans Peters and Paul van Husen—had also become involved.

Eventually, when the loosely formed group was discovered, the Nazis named them the Kreisau Circle (in German, *Kreisauer Kreis*), but among themselves they were known simply as the "friends."

At Moltke's insistence, they operated within strict confines of secrecy to avoid the danger of detection. Only Moltke and Peter Yorck knew the full extent of the group's involvement. The members worked in small groups, each one on a particular policy area. In this way, every member knew as little as possible about the other people involved. In some cases, they did not even know one another's names. They met at night in small numbers in members' homes or during the day in government offices under the pretext of official business. On occasion, members also conferred with specialists of a particular area who themselves were not even aware of the group's existence.

As he became increasingly aware of the depravity that humanity was capable of, Moltke became convinced that a new republic must be based on the moral code of a solid religious foundation. He also believed that for the group's plans to succeed, it was crucial to win the cooperation of the Catholic bishops. In the summer of 1941, he sought out the bishop of Berlin, Konrad von Preysing, and began exchanges with him every few weeks. Preysing had been known from the early years of the Nazi Party to be opposed to the regime. He had written to the pope in January 1941 to ask for an appeal on behalf of German Jews. Preysing had also studied law in his early years, and Moltke found it useful to discuss with him some of the basic principles of the reform of the constitution. Under Preysing's auspices, an office with the bland title Relief Organization of the Berlin Diocese was opened up to help victims of the Nazis.

Moltke had also read with a sense of encouragement the text of three sermons that Bishop Clemens von Galen of Münster had given during the summer of 1941, condemning the killing of incurables. Informed by Preysing that Galen was intellectually limited and slow to realize the evils of Nazism (although this assessment has been contradicted elsewhere), he was doubly impressed with the bishop's forceful words. It did not take long for Moltke to discover, however, that the German Catholic bishops were, as a collective body, paralyzed in opposing the Nazi system.

There were complex historical reasons for the logjam the bishops found themselves in when they met for their episcopal meetings that took place annually in Fulda. Kulturkampf, with its discriminatory actions toward Catholics, loomed large in their collective memory, and they insisted on the importance of Catholic allegiance to the state, especially since the Nazis had gained power through legitimate means and thus constituted the lawful authority. In the early days, the bishops had strongly denounced Nazism's pagan ideology, and some of them were harassed and pelted with rotten vegetables by Nazi-incited crowds, but they toned down their condemnation when they became aware that the Vatican approved of Hitler's anti-Bolshevism. They were also limited by the 1933 concordat to speaking out only on Church matters. Although the encyclical *Mit brennender Sorge* had been issued at the bishops' urging (the main author was one of their own number, Michael von Faulhaber, the cardinal archbishop of Munich), now that Germany was at war and Catholic soldiers were swearing oaths to Hitler, the bishops considered it their duty to promote patriotism. Above all, despite heated disagreements among themselves and individual statements against certain acts of injustice, they wanted to stand united. The result was a boiling-down of their common voice into an insipid Catholic leadership in the struggle against Nazism.

Moltke had therefore been looking for someone with inside influence to coax the Catholic hierarchy into action through solidarity with his group. When he answered the knock at his door on that October evening in 1941, he saw a slightly disheveled man in his late forties who introduced himself as a Jesuit priest. He invited Rösch into the tiny apartment, and thus began the Jesuit involvement in the Kreisau Circle. Two days later, Moltke made an assessment of Rösch in a letter to his wife, Freya: "A peasant's son with an outstanding head, skillful, educated, sound. I liked him very much." Here was his liaison with the wider Catholic Church, and he was delighted: "As far as I can make out he has only the top Jesuit in Rome above him." [2]

Plans were under way for a weekend gathering of the group at Moltke's Kreisau estate in Silesia the following May to discuss the theme of education and the relationship between church and state. Rösch was invited to attend and to make a presentation on the Catholic position. The intent of the weekend meeting was to provide an extended period for the group to discuss a particular subject; and an invitation to an estate far off the beaten track, under the guise of a weekend party, was not likely to arouse suspicion. (A dicey situation did arise at the meeting, however, in the presence on the estate of a Nazi relative of Moltke's, a woman who kept asking Freya von Moltke why so many men were visiting. The woman insisted there was something wrong; it did not seem an innocuous group. Moltke's wife gave a nonchalant wave, insisting they were just men from her husband's work.)

During this gathering, or soon afterward, Moltke had an additional question for the Jesuit provincial. He himself was familiar with the papal encyclicals that had established the Catholic position on social justice, *Rerum Novarum* and *Quadragesimo Anno,* but the group needed an expert on these documents. Did Rösch know of such an expert?

One person came immediately to Rösch's mind: the rector of the small church of St. Georg in Munich's sleepy suburb of Bogenhausen, Alfred Delp.

Delp's Involvement at Kreisau

The details of Delp's decision to join the Kreisau "friends" are not known, but several months earlier he had made clear where he stood on the matter of resistance: "Whoever doesn't have the courage to make history," he wrote, "is doomed to become its object. We have to take action."[3]

At the end of July 1942, Delp was on his way to Berlin, and at the beginning of August he was immersed in the preparatory meetings for the second Kreisau gathering. Rösch and a third Jesuit, Lothar König, who had been a professor of cosmology at the Jesuit college in Pullach before its close, also came to the meetings. König, a year older than Delp and trained as a scientist, was precise and well organized, and he held a great deal of information behind a calm and reticent exterior. Among the three of them, important links with various members of Germany's Catholic hierarchy were ensured. In particular, Rösch kept up close contact with Faulhaber and Delp with Bishop Johannes Dietz of Fulda, who had initiated the Mission to Men conferences. König acted as a courier between bishops, carrying clandestine news from one to another.

The Jesuits' task at these preliminary Kreisau meetings was to establish common ground between the churches and the Social Democrats and trade unionists. They took as their starting point the social encyclicals, which made clear the Catholic position that economic life must be safeguarded by just laws. To everyone's surprise, a common understanding with hard-nosed socialists was reached more easily than they had predicted. One of the factors that served to unite all the participants in spite of their different backgrounds—who in other times and under different circumstances might have been downright antagonistic to one another—was a common disillusionment with the two types of socialism they encountered, far-left Bolshevism and far-right Nazism. In both

Lothar König. *Courtesy of the Archives of the Upper German Province of the Society of Jesus (Archivum Monacense SJ), Munich.*

ideologies, all individuality was subsumed into a collective mass, and human beings became mere machines.

In mid-October 1942, Delp traveled by train to Breslau and from there through the lush pastoral Silesian countryside to the Kreisau estate, the sole Jesuit participant at the second weekend gathering. On his arrival, he was greeted by Moltke and his wife, who had made arrangements for the guests to be properly fed by saving up tokens from ration cards. Delp was led past the *schloss,* the main house of the estate, where two elderly aunts of Moltke's lived, along a tree-lined pathway and across two streams, past cows and chickens, to the *berghaus,* a more modest house that was home to Moltke, his wife, and their two small sons. Some of the guests were housed at the *berghaus* and others at the *schloss.* The *berghaus* had a wide veranda overlooking the estate's fields and a range of blue and

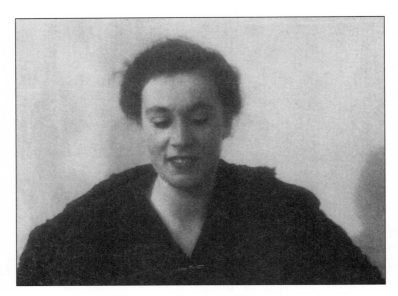

Freya von Moltke. *Courtesy of Freya von Moltke.*

gray mountains. The meetings took place in the elegant, airy parlor of the *berghaus;* they began with presentations of papers, followed by discussion, an attempt at consensus, and preparation of a final document. The theme of the weekend was the structure of the state and the economy. Ten people participated, including Moltke, his wife, and Peter Yorck's wife, Marion.

More than fifty years later, Freya von Moltke remembered Delp as having health problems (at the time, he was afflicted with a serious staph infection that caused painful boils), and yet in spite of his discomfort he brought liveliness, humor, and a sense of serenity to the group. Others have similarly recalled him as bringing a spiritual depth to the group's meetings. A certain lightheartedness tempered the seriousness of purpose and the psychological tension created by the extreme secrecy of the occasion. The group held a common conviction that their purpose was right and necessary. Discussions were animated and lasted well into the night; Delp reveled in the atmosphere of ecumenical openness and the exposure to other points of view. On Sunday, all went to their respective churches before resuming their discussions; Delp said Mass in the nearby Catholic church.

In the discussions, the participants were bound together in mutual trust, knowing that after they had returned to their respective worlds, something said in an unguarded moment could mean imprisonment and death. In a time of peace, people with such diverse backgrounds might have found too many obstacles in their way of understanding, but now, their willingness to risk everything, including their lives, united them in friendships that transcended lines of class, belief, and background. For Delp, the experience was exhilarating.

Munich Bombing

Almost immediately after his return to Munich from the rustic setting of Silesia, Delp found himself face to face with yet another reality of war: air raids. From October 1942 onward, Allied bomb attacks became part of the fabric of life in Munich: the piercing sirens, the frantic rush for shelter in the basement, where the occupants of the parish house huddled, sang hymns, prayed together, and told jokes to relieve the anxiety. The roar of the planes and the explosions sounded louder and louder overhead, the foundation shook, the smoke penetrated the basement walls. And then, the aftermath: the tentative emergence from below, handkerchiefs pressed to faces against the clinging smell of smoke and dust and gas; the sky red with flames; crumbled heaps of debris where buildings stood moments before; the deadly stillness.

Delp became known for his mechanical skills and for his fearlessness in the face of the bombing raids: after the sounds of the planes had died away, he often left the basement before the all-clear signal, rushing from one demolished house to another, digging and sifting to reach those buried beneath the rubble. He reportedly took over the rescue operation after one attack, yelling orders to the men from the fire department who were supposed to be in charge. This overenthusiastic effort earned him an official warning. In one letter he wrote, "Thank God that we've come through so well. . . . The church and house are again without roof, windows, doors, etc., there are deep cracks in the walls. . . . There's always something burning in the city. So many valuable places have burnt, the most beautiful churches, the most beautiful houses, all burnt. Whole streets and quarters have burnt. So many friends have been left with nothing."[4]

And then there was the necessity of resuming normal activities with little sleep and edgy nerves in the face of almost daily disaster: bloodied corpses, coffins piled one upon another, prayers for the dead repeated over and over, one funeral after another. Eventually, water and sewer lines were struck, the stench along the streets became unbearable, and electrical outages became commonplace. And for Delp and the others working against the Nazi regime, daily work was done with continual glances over the shoulder in the knowledge that an incautious word might mean imprisonment.

Work with the Catholic Hierarchy

Most German citizens were unaware of the resistance work that was going on in the army, the foreign office, and elsewhere by the end of 1942, but in spite of the obvious roadblocks and dangers, the clandestine networks quietly spread. Moltke tried to make the

Allies aware of the growing resistance movement during his travels to Switzerland and Norway on Abwehr business, and on one occasion he was accompanied by Dietrich Bonhoeffer, who had become employed by the Abwehr. (Moltke's many efforts to get Allied recognition of the German resistance movements proved to be in vain.) Delp and König established bonds with Catholic movements, and Delp connected the Kreisau group with two other resistance groups, a circle of Bavarian Catholic laypeople known as the Sperr Circle and the Catholic workers' movement in Cologne. The Bavarian group, organized by Franz Sperr, a former Bavarian envoy to the government in Berlin and a member of Delp's parish, helped to plan the urgent practical matters of regional leadership in the face of what they presumed would be an army takeover and a subsequent collapse of the regime.

The Cologne group, under the leadership of Bernhard Letterhaus and Nikolaus Gross, was aware early on of the dangers of Nazism. As early as 1930, Letterhaus had cut against the grain of general Catholic fear of Bolshevism by pointing out that the swastika, a perversion of the Christian cross, signified the more serious threat to the German people. Gross, originally a miner, had become the editor of the Catholic labor movement's newspaper. After the publication was banned, he continued to distribute pamphlets that were obliquely critical of the regime.

By now, rumor had filtered into the Kreisau group that the Jews who had been deported from Germany to camps in Poland were being systematically murdered by the thousands. The hearsay had seemed too far-fetched to believe, but in October 1942, Moltke heard the truth directly from a government administrator in Poland: the outrageous rumors were correct. This new knowledge brought a sense of particular urgency to the work of the group and the Christian consciences of its members.

All along, the three Kreisau Jesuits—Rösch, König, and Delp—had been prodding the bishops to publicly condemn Nazi policies. Moltke still kept in touch with Preysing in Berlin, who, he noted, had become worn down with anxiety over the bishops' inability to make strong collective statements. Indeed, the bishops had debated heatedly during their August 1942 conference about whether to make a public condemnation of the Nazi treatment of the Jews. Adolph Bertram, the eighty-three-year-old chair of the conference and the cardinal archbishop of Breslau, wanted absolute proof of the death camps. Bertram had vivid personal memories of Bismarck's Kulturkampf, and more than anything he wanted to underscore Catholic loyalty to the Fatherland by accommodating the state in matters that did not directly affect the Church.

By now, however, the Nazi persecution of the Catholic Church, begun in near stealth, had moved into full force: religious houses were closed, churches confiscated, priests incarcerated by the hundreds in the Dachau concentration camp. Speak out on behalf of Catholicism, the bishops decided. Continue resisting in clandestine ways. Beyond that, keep silent. Deeply frustrated, Preysing predicted that he and his fellow bishops would be harshly judged in the future for their collective failure to speak out in forceful terms against Nazi barbarities.

Moltke, bolstered by enthusiastic Jesuit approval, urged Preysing to brave it alone in a pastoral letter that would shock the Catholic public with specific details about the deported Jews. Preysing agreed, but the final draft of his letter, issued in December 1942, turned out to be a toned-down version of what the Kreisau people had hoped for. The letter, Moltke wrote, was "good, but not very good and not very emphatic. It is aimed at those who can hear, not at the deaf."[5] Among those who could hear, however, were members of the Nazi regime who objected to such lines as, "It is never permitted to take away human rights from members of alien races."[6] The deaf, of course, were the Catholic public who by and large looked to the hierarchy for leadership.

Other Resistance Groups

At the beginning of 1943, one resistance group did come to public attention. The White Rose, a small group of Munich students, had begun clandestinely distributing leaflets exhorting German citizens to rise up against the atrocities of the Nazi regime. When the German army finally surrendered at Stalingrad on February 3, 1943, and the end of the war seemed imminent, the students stepped up their protest, painting *Nieder mit Hitler* (Down with Hitler) and *Freiheit* (Freedom) on the walls of public buildings. In an act of giddy abandon, they scattered leaflets from the third floor of a university building into an inner courtyard; three students were immediately arrested, the brother and sister Hans and Sophie Scholl and Christoph Probst. The three were quickly tried and, on February 22, were beheaded.

Their daring final action had taken place only steps from Delp's former residence at *Stimmen der Zeit*. It is not known to what extent Delp was aware of the students' activities, but it seems that a meeting had been arranged between him and a philosophy professor by the name of Kurt Huber, who had been encouraging the students. The meeting never took place, and Huber himself was tried and executed the following July.

Nothing more is known about the circumstances regarding this aborted effort to link the White Rose with the Kreisau group. Moltke had certainly become aware of the students' activities and had taken a copy of one of their leaflets on a trip abroad as proof of German resistance, and he may have suggested that Delp contact them. It is also possible that Delp and Huber were acquainted with each other through Delp's preaching. Some have speculated that had the two groups met, they might have complemented each other well, with the steadiness and caution of Moltke's group tempering the White Rose's youthful rashness, and the zeal of the students injecting passion into the Kreisau group's intellectual activity.

More and more, however, the Kreisau group forged links with other resistance groups in an increasing awareness of the need for readiness. The heavy losses in Russia indicated that the army's reserves were near an end; the numbers of murders piling up in the name of the German people—in the Polish concentration camps, in the German camps, on the streets, in prisons—revealed a society decayed to the crumbling point; an Allied invasion was expected at any time; and there was now open talk within resistance circles that disillusioned army generals were set to overthrow the regime.

One such link came about with another circle of resisters known as "Goerdeler's group." The central figure of this group, Carl Goerdeler, a man in his late fifties, had as the mayor of Leipzig protested the treatment of Jews, and had resigned his position when the Nazis destroyed the town's statue of the Jewish composer Felix Mendelssohn. Goerdeler was fearless in his opposition to Nazism and was held in such high regard in the wider resistance movement that it was generally understood that with the end of Nazism, either by a coup d'état or by an Allied victory, he would become chancellor of Germany. Because the Kreisau members had set about the task of building a new constitution, they desperately wanted the two groups to come to an agreement.

At a meeting in Berlin at the end of 1942, with edgy nerves, frayed tempers, and exhausted bodies playing a part—in addition, perhaps, to an increased impatience that the war showed no sign of letting up—Delp came to verbal blows with a representative of

Goerdeler's group. The immediate and specific disagreement took place over a question of trade unions—the Kreisau group sought to get the masses on the side of the elites, mostly intellectuals, who were leading the opposition to Hitler, and trade unions were considered an important means to achieve this end. But this conflict merely reflected the fundamental differences between the two groups.

Foremost among these differences was Goerdeler's personal style: he tended to be indiscreet, taking little care to cover his tracks, writing notes and lists of names (the Kreisau members kept almost nothing in writing, knowing that a name kept in an inadvertent place could cost a life); and he was inclined to operate alone rather than in consultation with others. He was reputed to be a good speaker but not much of a listener. Most important, however, Goerdeler and his group were on the whole a full generation older than Moltke's group, and the age difference reflected an important difference in worldviews. Goerdeler's group looked back fondly on pre-World War I Germany, with its aristocratic and monarchical social order; the members of this group favored a restoration. The Kreisau group realized that Europe had irrevocably changed and that a break had to be made and a new foundation laid. From that new foundation, a new society would be built. The Kreisau move was toward peaceful revolution rather than restoration. Moltke wanted a federation of European states, not a plan just for Germany. The two groups' names for each other reflected with grim humor the disdain each had for the other's ideas: Goerdeler's group became known as "their excellencies" to the Kreisau members, and the members of Moltke's group were called "the young turks" by the older group.

A stormy follow-up meeting in early 1943 on foreign policy, at which Delp was not present, indicated little chance of the two groups coming to a fundamental agreement. Heightening the tension was the increased expectation within resistance circles that the army would soon stage a coup d'état. In that event, the Kreisau group's plan was to have a constitution and provisional government ready, complete with people prepared to take over the various responsibilities.

As the weeks wore on with no hint of an army coup d'état, tempers became even shorter and patience wore thin. "Why can't people have patience?" Moltke complained in a letter to his wife in early March. "Even König and Delp, who really should have learnt, from their discipline, to wait, are incapable of it, and when an action is followed by an inevitable setback, they become restless and don't see that beyond the valley is another height."[7] Two attempts were made on Hitler's life in March, both bombs failing to explode, and the army generals within the resistance movement continued to remain inert.

In April 1943, as plans were underway for the third Kreisau weekend meeting, Moltke's workplace, the Abwehr, which employed many resistance workers, began to come under close Gestapo inspection. Hans von Dohnanyi, a Kreisau member, was arrested along with his brother-in-law, Dietrich Bonhoeffer, and others. Moltke began to wonder if he should find another job as cover for his resistance work.

The third Kreisau weekend, however, took place in June as planned. Once again, Delp traveled to Kreisau and met with ten others to discuss foreign policy, which, in effect, meant the question of whether Europe would want to join in a federation with a restructured Germany. As at every meeting, all the papers except the most important were burned immediately after discussions, and no one saw the proposals or the final documents in written form. The most important papers were hidden by Freya von Moltke, along with her husband's letters, in the Kreisau beehive.

This meeting was the last of the Kreisau weekends. The country's postwar constitution, according to the Kreisau vision, was complete. Germany would be divided into local units, each of which would elect a representative to a national council, which in turn would elect the country's leaders. The country was to have a combined socialist and free-market economy, with the government owning the major industries. Trade unions were to be active in the work of private industry. The education system was to be completely reorganized and purged of Nazi ideology. Christianity was to provide the government's guiding principle, although citizen rights were to be given to people of all races and religions. Once the Nazi government was overthrown, by whatever means, a constitution could now be offered to the new leaders as at least a starting point in the reconstruction of the country.

Delp's particular contribution to the Kreisau constitution was evident in the prominence of labor and other social concerns in the documents. He had also, however, provided an important philosophical and religious framework on which a future society should be built. For Delp, a renewed religious sensibility—too long ignored within the modern economic and technological morass of alienation—was crucial: a sensibility in which all human beings would recognize themselves as made in the image of God, and in this recognition they would act accordingly in the world.

The Jesuits were unsuccessful, however, in drawing the Catholic bishops as a collective body into the work of the Kreisau group. A working draft of the bishops' 1943 pastoral letter, which condemned "the killing of incurables, innocent hostages, prisoners, and people of alien race and descent," was presented at their annual meeting in August and was rejected as too explicit.[8] Preysing complained to Moltke that the final draft "has been dry-cleaned, the last spots removed, and the colour too."[9] With varying degrees of

Alfred Delp, around 1943. *Courtesy of the Archives of the Upper German Province of the Society of Jesus (Archivum Monacense SJ), Munich.*

openness and courage, most of the bishops continued to act against the regime within their own dioceses. But because they differed so widely in their individual approaches to resistance, they found themselves incapable of anything more than pale compromise in their collective pronouncements. As a group, the bishops looked to the Vatican for leadership, which was not forthcoming. And in the end, they not only refrained from speaking out about the atrocities committed on the specific groups mentioned in the working draft of their 1943 letter, they also remained publicly silent about the acts of injustice committed by the Nazis on millions of Catholics, including incarcerated priests, slave laborers from Poland and Ukraine, and, eventually, the Kreisau Jesuits themselves.

CHAPTER 5

THE BEGINNING
OF THE END

January–July 28, 1944

In January 1944, Moltke was arrested and sent into protective custody at a prison attached to the Ravensbrück concentration camp. His resistance work had not yet been discovered; rather, it was an incidental episode that brought him to the attention of the authorities. A Gestapo agent managed to infiltrate a group of anti-Nazis, and Moltke phoned a colleague to warn him that he was under watch, not realizing that the man's phone was already tapped. (Some sources also claim that Moltke's name was revealed by a prisoner under torture.)

After Moltke's arrest, the Jesuits' contact with the Berlin core of Kreisau members dwindled, although König kept up communications with some of the Berlin group. For Delp, two more personal and more profound situations arose during these months.

By early 1944, he had lived almost eighteen years as a Jesuit and had not yet made final vows. Normally, one was admitted to final vows after about sixteen years in the Society of Jesus. Before final vows were taken, however, one had to pass through a process known as *Informationes,* a confidential procedure by which the provincial superior and his consultants might raise doubts about a candidate's suitability. In Delp's case, the *Informationes* produced sufficient doubts about him that Rösch informed him sometime in 1943 that his final vows were to be deferred to August 15, 1944.

There is no certainty about what transpired in the course of this matter; the *Informationes* remain confidential indefinitely. Thus, only conjectures are possible. Fellow Jesuits were aware of "questions of obedience and behavior" that bothered the provincial superior; Rösch had always perceived Delp as too independent, tending to act without proper permission, and this perception increased (perhaps justifiably) during the years that Delp lived at St. Georg's, apart from a Jesuit house.[1] In addition, Delp was said to have "an extravagant manner"; his cigar-smoking joie de vivre may have given the impression of unseemly worldliness, especially in the face of wartime austerity.[2] Also, a letter from Moltke to his wife mentions that to have a meal at the Jesuits' was to eat "like princes,"[3] and with some astonishment he relates in another letter the entire menu of a lunch provided by Delp, which he describes as a "state banquet": "bouillon with egg, venison with macaroni and dumplings, fruit tart, fruit and biscuits, and coffee."[4] If typical, a spread such as this, laid out days after Munich's first bombing raid amid a general food shortage, may have seemed rather lavish even to the generally well-fed Jesuits.

Delp also still displayed a certain stubbornness and impatience. The sharp critical attitude that had been noted in past years continued to make some of his fellow Jesuits dislike him. It also seems to be known that he suffered a personal crisis during 1941 and 1942, but no specifics are on record. There is speculation that it may have had something to do with either his vow of celibacy (he developed friendships with several women during his Munich years) or his vow of obedience (he may have felt this vow to be an impediment to his work in resistance). Or yet again, the dislocation he felt at the closing of *Stimmen der Zeit* and his move to St. Georg's may have begun to lead him in new directions. The parish had replaced the Society of Jesus as his community to some extent. Whereas some of his fellow Jesuits had shunned him because of his difficult personality, at St. Georg's he was warmly accepted and loved. He may have wondered for a time if there was still a place for him within the Society of Jesus.

The relationship between Delp and Rösch, always uneasy, had grown more complex as the war progressed. During his *Stimmen der Zeit* years, Delp lived close to Rösch's residence on Kaulbachstrasse, and they may have seen a good deal of each other in that period. There is much evidence that they respected each other's abilities and qualities of character, but inevitable clashes arose—Delp's vow of obedience clashing with his independent streak; Rösch's old-fashioned piety and religious style clashing with his knowledge of Delp's intellectual superiority and the obvious depth of his spiritual life. Delp's Protestant background provided him with a natural ecumenical openness that Rösch, schooled in Catholicism from infancy, did not possess to nearly the same extent. In their Kreisau involvement, the two shared both an intensity of purpose and a certain tendency toward recklessness, but the burden of responsibility Rösch carried in having brought Delp into this dangerous work likely heightened the complexity of his feelings toward the younger Jesuit. At any rate, the postponement of his vows brought Delp up short and placed in sharp relief his desire to be accepted by the Society of Jesus to the same degree that he had embraced the Jesuit way of life. He planned an eight-day Ignatian retreat in preparation for his final-vow day in August.

Another profound experience took place on June 13, 1944. That morning, after a vicious bomb attack on Munich, Delp rushed through the devastated streets of Bogenhausen in search of trapped people and came upon the ruins of the house belonging to one of his good friends, Maria Urban, the head teacher of a kindergarten attached to St. Georg's. This woman, known to her friends as "Urbi," was eventually found in the basement, killed by falling bricks and beams. Three days later (on the Feast of the Sacred Heart, as Delp later recorded), a friend of Urbi's who lived near Munich drove into the city and paid Delp a visit. She handed him an envelope that she said contained a letter Urbi had instructed the friend to give to Delp in the event of her death. The letter, which began in English, "Dear father" (the two had apparently practiced English together), had been written on February 15, 1943. In the letter, Urbi wrote that knowing of his important and dangerous work in resisting the Nazi system and realizing that he might one day be hunted down, imprisoned, and killed, she had asked God to take her life instead so that he might be spared to continue his work of resistance.

He slipped the letter into an inside pocket. The realization that Urbi had written it a full sixteen months earlier stunned him; there had never been any hint from her that she had made such a complete act of self-offering. No record exists of what Delp might have thought about Urbi's act of "substitute" oblation from a theological point of view, but the time for discursive thinking and speculative theology was fast running out. For Delp, it may already have been long past, and what touched him and continued to sustain him until his own life was offered up was Urbi's selfless act of the heart, an act given in complete abandonment and surrender.

Urbi's letter may have had a profound and lasting effect on him, but another event that had occurred a week earlier, on June 6, was to partly decide Delp's earthly fate. During the months since Moltke's arrest, Delp had become restless and edgy with no links to the wider resistance outside his own contacts. On this particular day, he traveled north to the town of Bamberg to give an evening lecture on the sources of confidence. After the lecture, he sought out a trusted person who agreed to lead him to a certain address. This person rode ahead of him on her bicycle, and according to a prearranged agreement, dropped her handkerchief as she passed by the house Delp wanted to visit.

It was the home of thirty-seven-year-old Count Claus Schenk von Stauffenberg, who was on a few days' leave from his job as chief of staff in the General Army Office in Berlin. The Kreisau members, aware that Stauffenberg had links with other resistance groups, had tried in 1943 to enlist his help in their work. Exactly why Delp chose to contact him again at this time is not known. It may have been an attempt to once again fit himself into some active resistance work.

Stauffenberg received the Jesuit graciously, but later reports from Stauffenberg's wife indicated that he was furious that Delp had come to his home, as clandestine visits put his young family in jeopardy. The two spent about an hour in discussion until Delp left to catch the train to Munich at half past eleven. Later, in his own deposition, Delp wrote that they talked in general terms about the state of Germany, the concerns of the bishops, and the relationship between the Church and the government. The visit may have also touched on the momentous event that had taken place early that morning—the long-awaited Allied invasion of Normandy.

Stauffenberg, who, like most of the resisters, knew to reveal only what was absolutely necessary, almost certainly did not inform Delp about what was foremost in his own mind—that another plan to assassinate Hitler was in the works, and that he himself was to be the assassin.

As months had dragged on into years, as the Nazis sank deeper into barbarism and German troops continued to fall, as bombs claimed civilian lives into the hundreds of thousands, leaving devastation in their wake, the question had come up time and again among the Kreisau members: Was the assassination of a tyrant morally justified? Charged as the atmosphere was with tension—secret meetings in cramped quarters, bomb scares, lack of sleep, news of the deaths of friends and loved ones—it was inevitable that the discussions, rather than taking place in any systematic way, lurched back and forth along various paths. There were moral stands on both sides: killing is always wrong regardless of the situation (Moltke held this line, arguing that his group was not justified in beginning a new society by following the murderous methods of the Nazis); but, ran the counterargument, countless murders have already taken place in the name of the German people and, therefore, the source of those murders must be stopped. There were practical questions: Will assassination achieve its desired purpose? Or will Hitler be mourned as a martyr? Will the Allies, having demanded an unconditional surrender, recognize a new German government following an assassination?

Among the Jesuits there were also differences: Rösch seems to have been against tyrannicide, Delp and König seem to have argued in favor. It is unlikely that any of them, even Moltke, held unwaveringly to one position or the other. As the likelihood of a revolt by the army generals receded, they gradually resigned themselves to the probability of a defeat from the outside rather than an overthrow from inside the country. But by 1944, most of the Berlin members of the Kreisau group, realizing that the Gestapo was gradually moving in on the various conspiracies, threw in their lot to one extent or another with Stauffenberg's plan. Of the three Kreisau Jesuits, cut off from the action in provincial Bavaria, only

König, through his Berlin contacts, seems to have known of the plan, and he may have given Delp some general information. Delp was ignorant of the specifics, however, and Rösch remained unaware of the entire plot.

On July 20, Delp spent the afternoon helping friends repair the roof of their house that had been damaged by the worst bomb blast yet, two days earlier. As usual, the blasts had gone on through the night, shaking the earth. But as Delp hammered the shingles, his shirtsleeves rolled up, his mood was lighthearted, and he made his usual jokes. Shortly before six o'clock, he left to visit his friends the Kreuser family. At half past six the radio broke the news: a bomb had been placed close to Hitler in a meeting room; the blast had killed several people, but Hitler himself had escaped with only minor injuries. Delp made little comment, but shook his head as if to indicate that the whole idea had not been a good one. No mention was made of the would-be assassin's identity. Delp went home and retired early.

Soon after midnight, Hitler came on the radio to assure the German people that he was still alive and that those who had perpetrated the attempt would be dealt with swiftly. For the first time, the chief culprit's name was revealed: Claus Schenk von Stauffenberg. In the Jesuit residence in Pullach, Lothar König heard Hitler's speech and hastened to the room of a fellow Jesuit, Franz von Tattenbach, urging him to get the news to Delp. Tattenbach found a bicycle, pedaled through the dark, and by half past three in the morning was in front of St. Georg's parish house, throwing stones at Delp's window. Delp did not respond. Then Tattenbach found a ladder, leaned it against the house and climbed up. Delp appeared at the window in his nightclothes, ready to do battle with a burglar: a comic-ironic scene, the beginning of the end.

As Hitler promised, action was swift. Stauffenberg and others were immediately shot by a firing squad, and in the next few days

Franz von Tattenbach.
*Courtesy of the Archives of
the Upper German Province
of the Society of Jesus
(Archivum Monacense SJ),
Munich.*

there was a general roundup of other suspects. Included were some
of the Kreisau group, Peter Yorck, Adam von Trott, and Hans-
Bernd von Haeften among them. Friends and fellow Jesuits cau-
tioned Delp about the danger he was in and advised him to go into
hiding. He refused on the grounds that he wanted to stay with the
people in Bogenhausen with whom he had suffered through the
many bombings and that he did not want to give the impression
that he knew more than in fact he did. Another reason: his August
15 final-vow ceremony, which he did not want postponed.

Delp's Arrest

Friday, July 28, a week after the unsuccessful attempt on Hitler's
life: eyewitness accounts remain of some of the final few hours of

Alfred Delp's freedom in the outside world. For the rest, it is possible to approximate a reconstruction; he had been practicing the same early morning discipline for the past eighteen years.

———

The sun rises in a yellow dusty haze over the crumbled heap that the city of Munich has become. The smell of charred, water-soaked ruins clings to the air. The Jesuit, dressed as usual in a suit and tie, emerges from the rectory and walks the short distance to the gate in the brick wall surrounding St. Georg's church. He opens the gate and enters the enclosed garden. In here is a sanctuary of peace, a holy place. The tiny church gleams in the early morning light, shaded somewhat by oak trees. The ugly bomb scars are still visible, but in some ways they seem inconsequential, a mistake.

He walks past the gray gravestones that are leaning this way and that, toward the side door that leads directly to the sacristy. The Mass vestments have been laid out, but he does not don them right away. Instead, he heads straight for the sanctuary, where the red tabernacle light is all that separates the church interior from semi-gloom. He genuflects, finds the light switch that turns on a single bulb, and kneels in the front pew, facing the altar. He makes the sign of the cross and is still for a moment. In front of him and on all sides, a fantasy of baroque excess fills the interior, all pink clouds and golden rays. An image of the church's namesake, St. Georg, rears his horse above the tabernacle, flanked by burgundy drapes and gilded marble columns. To his left, Our Lady as Queen of the World stands surrounded by saints and more saints, gazing up or gazing down, holding a staff, a book, a cross. And all around, there are cherubs with tiny wings: an exuberant contrast to the stark clergy world to which Delp belongs and to the world outside of hollow ruins and desperate people.

He opens his black breviary and recites the psalms for Lauds to himself in Latin: "Have mercy on me, O God, according to your steadfast love" (Psalms 51). When he finishes the psalms, he closes the breviary and remains in prayer. Meditation now makes up the better part of an hour. Today is the feast of four martyrs of the early Church, St. Nazarius and St. Celsus, St. Victor I and St. Innocent I, the last two of them popes. It may be that the focus of his meditation is the gospel of the day: "You will be betrayed even by parents and brothers, by relatives and friends; and they will put some of you to death. You will be hated by all because of my name. But not a hair of your head will perish. By your endurance you will gain your souls" (Luke 21:16–19). The final sentence of the gospel reading may bring a small smile to the face of the Jesuit, who tends to balk at the need for patient endurance, and perhaps he dwells on it awhile, asking God to allow this virtue to take deeper root.

People trickle into the church, the small core of daily communicants. He rises, genuflects, disappears into the sacristy to vest, then reemerges, the chasuble—red for martyrs—hanging stiffly down his back. The Mass begins: *"Introibo ad altare Dei. . . ."* ("I will go up to the altar of God. . . .") A few moments later, as he bows deeply over the center of the altar, reciting, *"Suscipe, sancta Trinitas . . ."* ("Receive, Holy Trinity . . ."), he may be aware that the door to the sacristy opens a crack and then softly closes again. It is the sacristan, a Vincentian sister. A friend, Ernst Kessler, has come with a note for him. The note will have to wait until Mass is over.

In the sacristy after Mass, the sister hands him the note. It is brief: a warning that the Gestapo is looking for him. He spends another few minutes in prayer. Small columns of smoke rise from the freshly extinguished candles. The faint, comforting fragrance of beeswax hangs in the air. He leaves the church by the sacristy door and lights the dead stub of a cigar. By now, the morning sun is shedding dappled light through the oak leaves onto the gravestones.

Outside the main door of the church, a young woman is waiting for him, the leader of a youth group. As they talk, two men approach. "Have I the honor of speaking with Father Delp?" asks one.

"Yes," says Delp.

"Can I speak with you a moment about an urgent matter?"

Delp answers, "I'm already with someone."

The man bows to the young woman and says, "I see you're busy, but the matter is very urgent."

Delp tells the young woman that he will see her again later. He leads the men through the gate and the three go into the parish house. The other inhabitants of the house wander about on edge, wondering what is happening behind the closed door of Delp's office. Outside, the parish secretary, Luise Oestreicher, and some others are clearing away bomb rubble. Eventually, Delp emerges from the house with the two men. He is wearing an overcoat. His face is gray and he looks ill.

"I'm under arrest," he says in a low, strained voice. "God be with you. Goodbye."[5] The three walk together toward a car on the street, and the car drives away.

In three days' time, the feast of the Jesuit founder, St. Ignatius of Loyola, will be commemorated. Where Delp is going, no gala celebration will mark the day. In two weeks, he is due to make his final vows in the Society of Jesus. That day will come and go, and no such event will take place. In six weeks, he will turn thirty-seven. He has slightly more than six months to live. In a letter to come, he will write of his life's education: the years as apprentice and journeyman are now over. The master's exam has just begun.[6]

CHAPTER 6

TEGEL PRISON

August–October 1944

What exactly happened in Alfred Delp's life over the next nine days is not known. The Gestapo car that carried him away from St. Georg's drove past one of the lovely parks flanking the Isar River, likely along the stately Maria-Theresiastrasse and across the Maximilian Bridge, where Delp may have caught his last view of the leafy river, with its gentle waterfalls, then through the half-bombed, hollowed center of the city, and finally to the Briennerstrasse. There, behind the Führerbau, where Hitler had signed the worthless Munich Agreement with Britain and France, the car stopped inside the grounds of the Gestapo headquarters at Wittelsbacher Palais, the most feared building in Munich.

Here, he may have been interrogated immediately, his accusers no longer displaying the exaggerated courtesy that had been shown outside St. Georg's. Or he may have been simply deposited in a small concrete cell, while officials dithered over what they should charge him with.

On the night of August 6, an acquaintance spotted Delp boarding a train to Berlin under guard. When the train arrived in Berlin in the early hours of August 7, a Munich friend, Dr. Fritz Valjavec, also caught sight of him and waited for him on the station platform.

Still under guard, Delp managed to whisper "Hapig" and "suitcase" to Valjavec as he passed by.

"Hapig" referred to a friend of Delp's, Marianne Hapig, a fifty-year-old social worker who was well known among the Berlin resistance circles for helping political prisoners and their families. It is not known whether "suitcase" referred to Delp's need for a change of clothes, because he had left St. Georg's with nothing but what he was wearing, or a certain suitcase in his room that contained damaging information.

From the Berlin train station, Delp was taken to Moabit, a Gestapo prison on the Lehrterstrasse. In the chilling atmosphere of this prison he stayed for the next seven weeks, enduring constant noise—the harsh barking of guards, the clatter of keys, the slamming and clanging of doors, the screams of other prisoners—and, for twenty-four hours a day, brilliant lights. Bombs rained down almost nightly, prompting at least one prisoner to call out, "Come closer!" in the hope of liberation in one form or another.[1] And from now until the end of his life, Delp was almost constantly in handcuffs.

From Moabit Prison he wrote his first letter, on August 9, to Sister Chrysolia Albrecht, long-time housekeeper at St. Georg's parish house. It was written on an official postcard and traveled through the normal postal system.

August 9, 1944

Dear Sister,

Please send me some underclothes (two sets), some handkerchiefs, some socks, and pajamas. Mark the whole thing "Urgent." I can be reached at the address over the page. All the best.

Fr. Alfred Delp

———

At this prison he underwent the euphemistically named "intensive interrogations." Fredrick the Great had abolished torture more than two hundred years earlier, but now that the failed July 20 assassination attempt had revealed a resistance movement, Hitler ordered that nothing be spared to bring the resisters to their knees and get information from them. By now, some of Delp's fellow Kreisau members had been tortured, tried, and executed, among them Peter Yorck, Adam von Trott, and Hans-Bernd von Haeften, and under a vicious "kith and kin" policy, relatives were also arrested. (All the wives of captured Kreisau members, with the exception of Freya von Moltke, were imprisoned and their children put into Nazi orphanages with name changes. None of them were ever brought to trial, however, and eventually, they were all reunited with their children.)

Prisoners were met with the usual "passive" torture: bright lights shining in their eyes at all hours, a meager diet of bread and water, and sleep deprivation—all of which were intended to wear down their resistance. Then there was verbal torture, often conducted by three officials, the first hurling abuse and obscenities, the second speaking in a soothing, obsequious voice, and the third appealing to prisoners' patriotism and code of honor. During this verbal interrogation, the prisoners often stood for hours, having had little sleep or nourishment. In Delp's case, the interrogators also attempted, by means that are not known, to persuade him to leave the Society of Jesus and join the Nazis.

And finally there was the overt, dreaded physical torture, which took various forms. In his prison writing, Delp speaks only obliquely of beatings. Others have written of heavy clubs, spiked leather straps, and whips of hippopotamus hide, all applied with such brute force that the handcuffed prisoner fell forward, face and head crashing upon the floor. The beatings continued for hours, until the naked flesh was a pulp, broken and bloody, and the prisoner had been driven delirious with pain. During these weeks, Delp's clothing, later picked up and washed by the two women who became known as the "two Mariannes," was stained with blood.

After the encounter with Delp at the train station, Valjavec had immediately contacted Marianne Hapig. She and a coworker, forty-six-year-old Marianne Pünder, had met Delp a year earlier in Munich. Now the two women set out on a prison search. In the meantime, St. Georg's secretary, Luise Oestreicher, had traveled to Berlin with the package of clothing he had requested. Finally, on August 14, Marianne Hapig discovered that Delp was imprisoned at Moabit, and she delivered his clothing the following day, which was to have been the day of his final vows. This marked the beginning of a clandestine contact with the outside world that continued until his death.

In a later letter, Delp described the treatment he had received the night before the clothing arrived. It had marked one of the lowest points of his long weeks in prison. After beating and humiliating him repeatedly, reducing their Jesuit captive to the helpless state of a wounded animal, his interrogators had thrown him back into his cell, jeering, "You're not going to be able to sleep tonight. You'll pray, but there'll be no God and no angel to deliver you. But we'll sleep well and tomorrow morning we'll have our strength back to give you another thrashing." [2] During the course of that night, he said, he had prayed that a bomb would fall on the prison, either killing him or setting him free, or that God would send him a sign that he had not been abandoned. He accepted the package of clothing from the two Mariannes as God's answer.

On September 27, the prisoners were ordered out of their cells and into the courtyard. The Lutheran pastor Eugen Gerstenmaier, a Kreisau friend and now a fellow prisoner, saw Delp standing behind him and turned to greet him. Delp stared through him as if he were a pane of glass. Two months of unmitigated misery had taken its toll.

Tegel Prison

After standing for hours in the courtyard, the prisoners were hustled into a prison vehicle and driven to northern Berlin, where they reached a building with two tall towers that looked like church spires. The vehicle slowed, a gate by the towers opened, and they passed into a courtyard with a maze of long prison blocks. This was Tegel Prison, a jail for ordinary criminals. Moabit, a prison for those charged with crimes against the regime, had become too damaged by bombs to keep the prisoners under tight security.

Inside the prison, the prisoners were led to a cellblock. Inside was a row of low iron doors, each with a peephole. The Tegel atmosphere was as cold and oppressive as that of the other jails, each cell equipped with a plank bed, a bucket, a washbasin, and a high barred window. Graffiti and dead insects plastered the walls. The foul smells of generations of inmates permeated the small space. They were kept in handcuffs at all times. However, Tegel was run by ordinary prison staff, who were less aggressive than the Nazi thugs, and it provided relief from the terror of Gestapo interrogations. Over the weeks, the prisoners even became somewhat friendly with some of the guards, and the guards, deliberately or not, sometimes fastened the handcuffs loosely so that the prisoner could work one hand free.

Delp soon discovered that Kreisau members were in adjoining cells: Moltke (who had been transferred from Ravensbrück) and Gerstenmaier on one side of him, and Josef Ernst Fugger, a Bavarian Kreisau connection, on the other. (He also shared Tegel with Dietrich Bonhoeffer for the last twelve days of the latter's stay there; Bonhoeffer's cell was in another part of the prison where more privileges were granted, so the two most likely never met.) Conversation was not allowed among the prisoners, but they were able to manage cryptic comments and code words during their daily exercise.

They settled into prison routine, with their fettered hands and their daily walk around the courtyard, and awaited word about their trials in the so-called People's Court, which had been hastily set up under the authority of Judge Roland Freisler in the wake of the July 20 assassination attempt. The most incriminating charge against Delp was that he knew about the plot against Hitler's life. Franz Sperr, the Bavarian leader of the Sperr Circle that Delp had kept in touch with, had visited Stauffenberg the same day as Delp and had apparently been aware of the plot. Under interrogation, he stated that Delp had been told about the plot as well. Nikolaus Gross, from the Cologne Catholic workers' association was also in custody and had made a similar statement about Delp. Knowing of the assassination plot and not reporting it to authorities was sufficient to incur the death penalty.

Three days after Delp's arrival at Tegel, the two Mariannes received their first letter from him, written on an official prison form. The letter sets the tone that carries through in all Delp's notes to them during the next four months: immediate practical requests and clearheaded strategizing for his upcoming trial, all intertwined with entreaties for union with him in prayer.

September 30, 1944

Good people,

Many thanks for getting my clothes to me in such a motherly way. And who would have thought that our holiday acquaintance would have been forced to bring forth such fruit? Please get me, if possible, a decent pair of shoes and a head covering (size 54-55) so that I can take my daily hour outside, even when it rains, etc. Greetings to my mother and everyone in Munich. And every day remind Urbi of her word. She has to keep it now. All the best and many thanks.

Alfred Delp

P.S. I'd almost forgotten the most important thing. I'm in Tegel Prison while investigations are going on for the People's Court. I'd never have dreamed this could be happening. I think it's about time you looked for a lawyer for me. I know too few people here. In Munich I heard the names Dix and Peter Schmitz mentioned. Be kind enough to give it some thought.

Thanks for everything.

Alfred Delp

Now that the Mariannes knew where Delp had been sent, they set out to work on his behalf once again. It was customary for friends and relatives to see to the prisoners' laundry and provide them with some food and personal items, such as soap and shaving supplies, which they would leave with guards at the prison entrance. The Mariannes quickly established this routine for Delp.

Each was a competent woman with a no-nonsense manner, and together they presented a fearless front. They also knew that cigarette bribes worked wonders on the prison staff. And so, not for the first time in the case of a Catholic priest, they immediately approached the head guard and sweet-talked him into allowing hosts and a small bottle of wine into Delp's cell so that he might say Mass. The guard relented, grumbling that he could get into serious trouble if caught and that he could not understand this religious type of prisoner—polite, refined, quietly praying and reading books—who stood out from the usual crooks and scoundrels inhabiting the Tegel cells.

The next day, October 1, Delp said his first Mass in his cell. The Eucharist thus became a lifeline for others in the prison through a method used perhaps by imprisoned priests everywhere: with his bound wrists, he knocked on his wall to the left and the right when Mass was beginning, and the others in turn knocked on their walls, and so on until the entire block of prison cells became alive with the great offering, the cosmic prayer of thanksgiving. Here, religious differences vanished. And gathered into the prayer, in the dank and putrid prison cell, came all the misery and the horror, the evil and the despair of all suffering humanity. For Delp and for his chained comrades, the Mass was not only a momentary consolation, a means of hanging on until the next day, but a meeting place of the world's sinfulness and the purifying presence of God.

Delp kept a consecrated host with him at all times in a specially made cloth holder; a round linen disk held the host and then was placed inside a white linen pouch, sewn with fine gold stitching, small and thin enough to be kept in an inner pocket. Like others before it, the pouch container had been blessed by Bishop von Preysing and given to the prison chaplain.

The chaplains—the Catholic Peter Buchholz and the Lutheran Harald Poelchau, who had been a Kreisau member himself—made regular visits to the prisoners. They brought reading material as well as welcome conversation and moral support into Delp's isolation, and they also provided the dangerous service of smuggling letters in and out. On October 13, the order came from the Gestapo that Delp, alone among the Kreisau inmates, was no longer to be allowed these visits. The exact reason for this added punishment is not known. It may have been an act of revenge for the fact that the other two Kreisau Jesuits, Rösch and König, had gone into hiding and so far had managed to elude capture, or it may have been another attempt on the Gestapo's part to persuade Delp to abandon the Jesuits.

The isolation was an additional suffering for Delp, but it was not long before two "mail routes" were devised. The first took place during the daily exercise when Gerstenmaier, whose cell was next to Delp's, walked either in front of or behind him. As they paraded around the yard, Delp managed with his manacled hands to reach into his jacket pocket, retrieve his letters, written in tiny script on small pieces of paper, and deposit them into Gerstenmaier's bound hands. Gerstenmaier then gave them to Harald Poelchau when the chaplain visited his cell.

The second route was through the Mariannes. A basket of clean laundry was delivered regularly to Delp, with a note written on an official order form, often in a light cryptic code. The basket also contained other supplies, such as shaving supplies, cigarettes, and food. Hidden deep into the folds of the clothing

Gestapo alert calling for the high-priority arrest of the fugitives Augustin Rösch and Lothar König on criminal charges. "Special Supplement to the German Criminal Police Bulletin," the headline reads. The document gives information on the background and identifying physical features of the two Jesuits and adds that they may be hiding in monasteries or in homes of people with church connections. *Courtesy of the Archives of the Upper German Province of the Society of Jesus (Archivum Monacense SJ), Munich.*

and among the supplies were pen, ink, and writing paper as well as incoming letters. When the two Mariannes picked up his dirty laundry, hidden inside and among the folds were Delp's outgoing letters.

The two women carried out this matter-of-fact delivery service as the city of Berlin disintegrated around them and the sharp eyes of the Gestapo continued to seek out traitors. Their daring action became Alfred Delp's lifeline.

CHAPTER 7

WITH BOUND
HANDS

October–November 1944

Delp's prison life settled into the routine of the terrible everyday. His long legs managed only three paces back and forth across the length of his squalid cell. The tedium of long hours was punctuated with moments of anguish, self-pity, grief over the worry he was causing his family (who had also learned that the youngest Delp son, twenty-four-year-old Fritz, was missing in action), physical pain from an abscessed tooth, and terror over the charges against him.

During the daily circle walk in the courtyard, Delp and his friends discovered that, though closely watched, when they came to the corner of the building, they could speak into it and their words would spring back in an echo to the people behind them. In this way, Delp learned the bits of news that the chaplains had been relaying to the others. It was all of the worst kind. Anyone connected with the July 20 plot in even the remotest way had been hunted down and those who were caught, like themselves, had been imprisoned, tortured, and charged with treason. Most of those already tried at the People's Court had been found guilty and hanged within hours of the verdict. Appeals were fruitless.

Familiar names cropped up in the roll call of the condemned. One was Herman Wehrle, a priest from the Precious Blood parish in Munich, whom Delp knew well. Under torture, a prisoner had named Wehrle, who, the prisoner said, had given him sacramental absolution even after he had told the priest he wanted to see Hitler killed. Wehrle was called to Berlin to testify at the man's trial and in a perverse blink of an eye had found himself on trial as well. He was hanged, Delp learned, on September 14.

More news of executions was to come, including, in November, that of Bernhard Letterhaus, one of the leaders of the Cologne Catholic workers' organization with whom Delp had established links.

Back in the isolation of his cell, mental torments oppressed and threatened to overwhelm Delp. He clung to his few consolations: the occasional friendly greeting of a guard; the surreptitious loosening of his handcuffs from time to time; the few moments in prayer when the clouds would briefly lift; his daily Mass; and the sight of the laundry basket with its hidden cargo of letters and blank paper.

As the weeks dragged on, Delp became more aware than ever of his fragile psyche, his tendency to give in to depression and despair. He knew he would not be able to endure without the knowledge that everyone who loved him was storming heaven on his behalf. He began to realize also how much of his pre-prison God-talk had been so much rhetoric, that his spiritual nakedness in the presence of God within the confines of his cell was of a new and terrifying order. And he needed to be assured as well that he was loved and cared for, particularly by the three groups of people he himself cared for the most: his family, his community at St. Georg's, and

Maria Delp. *Courtesy of Marianne Junk.*

his Jesuit brothers. He poured his longings and his needs onto the small sheets of paper in tiny, barely decipherable script.

Besides the two Mariannes, Delp's letters went to these three destinations, and in particular to his parents, Luise Oestreicher, and his fellow Jesuit Franz von Tattenbach. Luise Oestreicher, the thirty-four-year-old secretary of St. Georg's parish house, had by this time been conscripted for work in a Munich armament factory, but she still kept a close connection with St. Georg's parishioners and served as Delp's connection with the community that had come to mean so much to him over the previous three years. Tattenbach, two years younger than Delp, acted as a Jesuit courier between Munich and Berlin and became Delp's main link with the Society of Jesus. It is probably fair to say that whatever friendship with Tattenbach may have existed before Delp's arrest, a deep bond was created between the two during these months.

Other surviving letters were to various friends in Munich, including the Kreuser family, with whom Delp had heard the fateful news of the assassination attempt, and Fritz Valjavec, the man who had spotted Delp at the Berlin station. Delp used pseudonyms to sign his letters, partly as a joke and partly as a precaution in case of detection. His usual pseudonyms were "Max" for the two Mariannes, "Bullus" (a nickname from Stella Matutina days) for Tattenbach, and "Georg" for Luise Oestreicher. He did not date the letters; the dates were added later, possibly by the Mariannes, and so in many cases are only approximate.

To Luise Oestreicher, end of October 1944

Dear L.,

I'm back writing you a few greetings again. I don't know if they'll get to you. Actually, I know nothing about anyone except for the people handcuffed here, who are becoming fewer every day. "Unicus et pauper sum ego," or "I've become very alone and miserable," it says in a psalm. I'm so grateful for the Host, which I've had in my cell since October 1. It breaks the isolation, although, I'm ashamed to admit, sometimes I feel so tired and devastated that I can no longer grasp this reality at all.

Right now I need all my strength to cope with a toothache and the pain of sinus infection. I hope it won't fester. That's always been a nasty problem for me.

I can't write much to you today; it's not a good day. Sometimes one's whole destiny pushes itself together into a ton-weight and settles on the heart, and one really doesn't know how long this heart can be expected to take it.

I've still heard nothing from you. That's also very hard at the moment. How can all this go on?

I believe in God and in life. And whatever we pray for with faith, we'll get. Faith is the secret. And I don't believe that God will let me choke. . . . But I honestly can't say anything better than that about my situation. God has profoundly entrapped me and challenged me to keep my word from former times: with him alone can one live and deal with one's destiny.

How is everything with you? Greetings to all the dear ones. Wishing you God's blessing and fulfillment.

Georg

I'd appreciate a few Masses at St. Georg's, if that's possible. At any rate, I must now rely on the community of good people. My own strength has gone. "God alone suffices": I said that once when I was very self-sufficient. And look at me now. Until now I did everything in a false manner, and it got increasingly worse. So tell Tattenbach and Dold to pray hard in the Society. There's just nothing more they can do. If I were worth millions, some people would be able to get all the way to the top on my behalf, but I'm only a beaten and failed human being. May the walk across the tightrope be taken in God's name. Greetings to your family and to Johannes.

Also to Karl, Wessling, Laplace, Kessler, Chrysolia, Annemarie. Please send me news of the attacks.

To the Kreuser Family, mid-November 1944

Dear Friends,

In spite of my present situation, I have not forgotten the special name days this month. They have been remembrances of good and dear people, of loyalty and goodness, of many an hour spent in a welcoming home. And these have been days of prayer for God's protection and blessing on everyone. With my fettered hands I have blessed each one often. . . .

Yes, life has come to this. I have learned much in these twelve weeks of bitterness, temptation, and loneliness. And misery. Yet God is good enough to help me make use of it all. With his help I always have hope, yet in purely human terms things seem pretty hopeless. Between myself and the gallows lies nothing less than a miracle. Please pray and wait with me, and get the children to pray.

I imagine myself once again with hands that are free to open the door or shave myself or pick up a piece of bread—such rare priceless things. And each week we're becoming fewer. The will to destruction is hard and clear. The decisive hour is coming closer for us. At present the trial is set for the 7th or 8th of December.

I still have some wine, and on the 19th as in former years, I will say Mass. I have had this great grace of God since October 1. Since that date, I have had the Blessed Sacrament with me and I can celebrate Mass with my bound hands. At night, because the light is always on.

Thanks for everything. I hope the children are growing well. Special blessings to Karl-Adolf and Elisabeth. Don't go around talking about this letter. Please pray and hope. May God's protection be with my dear people.

A.

To Sister Chrysolia, mid-November 1944

Dear S.,

Greetings to you. Whether and how this will get to you, I don't know. If it does get to you, don't say much further about it.

I just want to thank you for all the work you've done for me. Thank the other sisters as well. And to apologize for all the trouble we went through together. Oh, how small and narrow all those things really were. How completely different the world looks after these ten weeks of terrible worry and hunger and pain and hopelessness!

Yes, and now I need your prayer. I think that we're sticking together now in the same way that we did in the basement, praying like mad together. I'm begging you now. I'm in a terrible state of affairs. If God doesn't help, I don't see any other way out. Please get the other sisters to pray too. Greetings to everybody in the house. Mid-December is probably when my fate will be decided. So many of my friends here have already died, but the "long Baron" is still alive.[1] We're going to be on trial together. Greetings to everyone, thank you for everything, and ask everybody to pray.

God bless you.

Your old patient

To Luise Oestreicher, November 17, 1944

Dear L.,

The decisive hour is inevitably creeping up. The possibility of a settlement beforehand has been cut off short. As things stand now, the hearing will be December 7 or 8. God has until then to work his miracle.

This week has in many ways been really turbulent. Three of our number have gone the way that remains a bitter possibility for all of us and from which only a miracle of God can separate and protect us. Inside myself, I have much to do, to ask, to offer up completely, before God. One thing is clear and tangible to me in a way that it seldom has been: the world is full of God. From every pore, God rushes out to us, as it were. But we're often blind. We remain stuck in the good times and the bad times and don't experience them right up to the point where the spring flows forth from God. That's true . . . for pleasant experiences as well as for unhappy ones. In everything, God wants to celebrate encounter and asks for the prayerful response of surrender. The trick and the duty is only this: to develop a lasting awareness and a lasting attitude out of these insights and graces—or rather, to allow them to develop. Then life becomes free, in that freedom which we have often looked for. . . .

I've just heard about the recent attacks in Munich. Please let me know how you and the friends are. It's really too much, this worry and uncertainty, on top of everything else.

Today is another hard day. God is dealing so intensely with me that he's making me rely on him totally. I've been in isolation now for some time. I should learn what believing and trusting mean. Every hour it's as if I'm learning this for the first time. There are also some good hours of fullness and comfort, but for the most part we're without any doubt on a tightrope and we have to walk across an abyss; and not only that, but snipers are shooting at us. And some of us are constantly falling off.

Some days I tell God that I'm a little bambino and I need some candy for comfort. He then responds to me in terrific ways. Recently, on one of these days the two Mariannes were able to get me twenty cigarettes and five cigars all at one time. And in the same way, the dear gray prayer book and a few things that tasted keenly of Munich. And sometimes I pray for a word of guidance and consolation, and so I break open the Scripture at random. I've just now opened it: Those who believe will do the following miracles. . . . Mark 16:16 ff. I tried it again, like a game, and this time it broke open at Matthew 20. Another word of confidence.

Oh, how restricted is the human heart in matters of its own ability: in hope and faith. It needs help to come to itself and not to flutter around like some shy birds that have fallen out of their nest because they've only half-learned to fly. Faith as a virtue is God's "Yes" to himself in human freedom—I preached that at one time. That's how it is now—exactly that. Pray and hope and believe with me that the Lord soon brings us poor Peters to the other side and once again sets us down on solid ground. But we no longer want to regard him quite as firmly as we sometimes did.

I wanted so badly to write something that hangs together. But reading material and everything else is so happenstance. Even that is a blessing, though. For the first ten weeks I had absolutely nothing. And then with these tied hands nothing much can be done in the way of writing. The few moments when they're free, they're incapable of doing anything. And it's dangerous to make pictures on the table with tied hands! But indeed the angel is here, and the Madonna. And God is in all things. . . .

And now, God bless you. All the best. Greetings to my friends. I'm really counting on you. Good-bye and God protect you.

Georg

To Marianne Hapig and Marianne Pünder, November 22, 1944

Good people,

For once I really have to try and get a word of thanks to you as well. Since the moment of decision is coming closer—as things currently stand, December 7 or 8—I have to expect just about anything. And I do, although I still keep believing in the miracle that stands between me and the gallows. It wasn't for nothing that Urbi's heart suffered for a whole year from the fear of death. She made her offering in connection with what's happening now. The date of her letter, February 15, 1943, is very consoling. And her sacrifice was accepted a few days after something else happened, which is my reason for being here. I have her letter here, with the Sacrament on top of it.

Good Pastor Gerstenmaier recently said to me while we were taking our "circus walk" in a circle—handcuffed and watched, but it's still possible—"I'd rather hope to death than perish in unbelief." *Ecce* [Behold]. . . .

God has taken me at my word and has placed me in the most extreme position possible. Regardless of anything, I have to say "Yes" a thousand times to him. That's sometimes a great strain on the heart, even from a purely physical point of view. These days, ever since the death of Letterhaus and the others, have been very hard. For myself personally, I see the situation as an intensive education in faith that God is giving me. The whole manner in which everything came about; the determination with which he knocked all the trumps out of my hand and let my self-assurance fall to pieces; the cruel twist in that finally, the statement which is most likely to lead to disaster is in fact wrong: all of this indicates that I must answer a specific question God is asking. It's a tough answer, because on the one hand it must be free with regard to the outcome of the situation, and at the same time it has to be given in hope.

I'm trying hard and discovering ever new sides to God; the world is full of God; God comes even in misery and there is encounter, the need for discernment, and also comfort and blessing. You've already given me so much help. The experience that a piece of bread can be a great grace is a new one for me. But above all, the realization that there are people nearby who care for me and are mindful of me is often a great consolation. And how often you have come right during the hours of depression. I'll never forget the first time, on August 14. I'd just asked Urbi if she could give me a sign. I was coming back right then from a terrible beating, smashed up, hopeless and helpless—and just then, totally unexpectedly, your good things came. The things in themselves are good news, but even more so is that the things bring news of people who break into my isolation.

Since the *Sanctissimum* [Blessed Sacrament] has been here, the world has become more pleasant again, and so I want to abandon myself to God's freedom and God's goodness and take pains not to refuse him in any way. And yet remain confident that he will bring us across the sea without allowing us to drown.

Thanks a lot for everything, and I'll see you again, one place or the other. And don't forget to pray and hope with me. All of it, however, is to be consecrated and blessed seed. The hours I've gone through up to now have been rich and, in the mystery of God, have been his will.

Your loyal and grateful

Max

To Luise Oestreicher, end of November 1944

Dear L.,

Many thanks for your greetings. I was so glad to hear from you. How are things going for you in the factory? Where is it? Is it reasonably safe from bomb attacks?

I'm fine. The verdict will probably be decided between the 8th and the 15th, or else the middle of December. Unless, which has often been the case, something happens in the meantime. God is right here "in the game" with me, even in spite of the logic that still seems inescapable. I'm counting on that.

During one night, around August 15, I was nearly in despair. I was brought back to the prison late in the evening, badly beaten. The SS men who brought me left with the words, "You're not going to be able to sleep tonight. You'll pray, but there'll be no God and no angel to deliver you. But we'll sleep and tomorrow morning we'll have our strength back to give you another thrashing." I was so relieved when the alarm sounded, and I expected the bomb to either kill me or allow me to escape. But neither happened. And during that night I saw that the whole fateful course of events was going to be as it later turned out. God has confronted me. Now it's up to me. I believe more and more firmly and confidently in the hand that takes us and guides us. . . .

I'm getting quite disgusting and always going on only about myself. That's how egotistical a person becomes as a "patient." Oh, how I'd like to help people who are suffering, yet I myself don't count as a person any more, but only as a number. Here in prison I'm number 1442, in cell 8/313. I wonder when I'll be addressed as Father Delp again?

Pray with me, in a valiant spirit. . . . Ask our friends to pray. God bless you. Thank you.

Georg

It's too bad that no one has attended to my family. They still don't have any idea what's happening or what it's all about. I'm now trying to get a letter to them along the same route as this one, since they're not allowing me to send or receive mail. This is a special friendly gesture like a variety of others, which nonetheless doesn't achieve its desired end. (Meanwhile, my hands have been bound again and I'm trying to scrawl something.)

How did Dold and the other priests at St. Michael's fare? Greetings to everybody.

Could it be that the various people in Munich don't have contact with each other? Well, that's actually not so important. Help me, so that all eight of us will persevere with prayer and faith. Because if one of us fails, life is no longer nice for the rest. Do you believe there'll be a miracle? Why have you sidestepped my question? All the best.

Georg

To Friedrich and Maria Delp, end of November 1944

Dear Mother, dear Father,

Perhaps it's going to be possible to get news to you somehow. I can imagine the awful worry you must have, especially not knowing exactly what's happening. I wish I could have spared you this worry as much as, and even more than, I wish I could have spared myself this trouble.

My arrest is connected to the July events. I knew some of the people who were involved, and I'm accused of knowing about the plans beforehand and not reporting them. Of course this is a very serious charge, and it's very worrisome. But we don't want to lose courage, but rather trust in God, who has always been there to help us.

I'm placing all my trust in God and asking very much for your prayer. As things look now, the trial will likely be in mid-December, and if so you'll certainly be informed at that time.

In the meantime, keep well, and God's rich blessings to you. I have a good feeling that Fritz will be found. So bear up, dearest parents, and stay steadfast under all this hardship and burden.

Forgive me for all the worry I'm causing you and thank you for all the countless good you've done for me. God bless you. Greetings to my brothers and sisters.

Alfred

To Dr. Fritz Valjavec, November 1944

Dear Friend,

Thanks very much for your devoted kindness. We certainly imagined our "teamwork" to be something different. But perhaps it will still happen. Although I'm clear about the situation, I believe in God as the God of destiny. And in spite of everything, I've had a good feeling during these nineteen weeks, and I still have. . . .

All the best to you, good luck with your work and plans, and God's fruitful and protective blessing on you and your family.

Thank you.

Delp

CHAPTER 8

ACROSS THE ABYSS

December 1–December 7, 1944

By the beginning of December, Delp's mind was taken up with his life's immediate task: his defense. The trial was planned for December 8 and 9, but word filtered through that it might be postponed. The legal process was not a straightforward one: legal counsel was assigned to him, but there were strict limits on his access to the lawyer. As Delp became increasingly acquainted with his lawyer, his initial enthusiasm for a fair legal process began to wane. The lawyer seemed only to go through the motions with little interest in the case.

And then there was the matter of the most serious charge against him: Delp's visit to Stauffenberg, which supposedly proved his knowledge of the plot against Hitler. The work he had been actually engaged in all along—helping to plan a renewed postwar Germany—paled, in Nazi eyes, beside the treasonable act of aiding an assassin.

He was aware, too, that the decision of Rösch and König to go into hiding would probably be held against him. Their disappearances had likely been thrown at him during interrogations: if the Bavarian Jesuits were innocent, why had the other two disappeared? He may have felt abandoned by his two fellow Jesuits. The three had been bound together in a particular way because of their dangerous work, and now he alone was facing the final consequence.

Still in isolation, Delp became preoccupied with the attempt to have Nikolaus Gross and Franz Sperr retract their statements that he had been told beforehand about the plot. Gross, the man from Cologne, seemed to understand the gravity and falseness of the accusation against him and was prepared to retract, but Sperr, in Delp's mind at least, seemed to have erected a mental barrier to the question. Compounding the situation was the overwhelming physical difficulty of communicating with Sperr, who was being held in another prison. Tattenbach and the Mariannes were Delp's only reliable means of working up a proper defense, and, with their help, he scoured the network of possibilities for further help. Perhaps his writing, articles, and books, might offer a glimpse into his thinking; any right-thinking judge could see they were not the product of a treasonous mind. Could a way be found to present Heinrich Himmler (the head of the Gestapo and, next to Hitler, the most powerful man in Germany) with Moltke's postwar plans? These plans were, after all, the best possible means of transition back to a sane society. Could help be found through Hermine Hoffman, the Nazi aunt of one of the Jesuits (whom the Jesuits nicknamed "Hitler's Mother" and who often used her connections to help imprisoned priests)?

News of his family also brought continual concern. His two soldier brothers, at least, were safe for now, having both been captured and sent to American prisoner-of-war camps. But a bomb had damaged his parents' home in Lampertheim the previous May, and, though they had escaped injury, his father, by this time bedridden, had been placed in a nursing home. His care had drained the family's meager finances. In early December, his mother moved with his sister Greta's six-year-old daughter, Marianne Kern, to

Munich, while Greta stayed behind at a compulsory factory job in Lampertheim. In Munich, grandmother and grandchild lived with the Kreuser family for a time and then moved on to the greater safety of rural Wolferkam, where Delp had spent such happy vacations. Maria Delp desperately wanted to travel to Berlin to visit her imprisoned son, but he refused to allow it because of the fear that the "kith and kin" policy might lead to her arrest as well. And he continued to worry about the fatherless Marianne, lest she become overly coddled and spoiled.

As for the starkness of his everyday existence, his reflections grew ever deeper. He recognized his prison cell and the upcoming trial as a testing ground. An abyss lay before him; the way across did not depend on his own prowess as it might have done in the heroic stories of his youth, but rather the complete opposite: what was demanded of him now was nothing less than a total surrender to the loving mercy of God. He was able to pinpoint the moment when he first let go of his misery and heaved himself into God's care: it was the night he had received the most savage of the Gestapo beatings and insults and had been deposited back in his cell, a mass of blood and bruises. He found comfort in the Gospel figure of Peter, who flailed about in the water whenever he relied on his own strength and who walked in safety only when he surrendered himself in trust. With grim humor, Delp employed a circus metaphor to describe his situation—the way the prisoners were paraded like animals on their daily exercise round, the arena-like trial that lay ahead, and the minute-by-minute walk across the tightrope.

The kinship that had begun during the clandestine meetings of the Kreisau group now deepened into spiritual union, made all the more intense by the furtiveness of their communication. Through signs and whisperings they shared in one another's prayer, and Delp introduced his Protestant colleagues to some of his favorite

Catholic devotions. Besides daily Mass, in which they participated by means of the coded knocking on walls, he led them in novenas.

The Meditations

Other creative energies were released at this time as well. In his letter to Luise Oestreicher dated November 17, he referred to "the dear gray prayer book" that she had sent him.[1] This small prayer book contained prayers and devotions, among them the Litany of the Heart of Jesus, that Jesuits had been given in the novitiate. This particular litany may have been a favorite of Delp's. In earlier times, he had regarded the heart of Jesus as the preeminent symbol of God's love and, in his sermons, had preached love as the only path to God. It also struck him as providential that Urbi's self-offering had come to him on the Feast of the Sacred Heart. It can easily be imagined that as his manacled hands thumbed through the small gray book with its familiar prayers redolent of certain people and places, he came upon this litany and began reading the invocations with new eyes and deeper understanding: "Heart of Jesus, Son of the eternal Father; Heart of Jesus, formed by the Holy Spirit in the womb of the Virgin Mother; Heart of Jesus, substantially united to the Word of God. . . ."

In a letter dated December 1, he told the Mariannes he was writing a reflection each day on each of the litany's invocations, and in the same letter he asked for more ink. Delp was highly critical of the devotion to the Sacred Heart—as he was of much of the Church's prayer life as it was popularly practiced—because of the sugarcoated sentimentality that tended to smother its rich symbolism and profound meaning for human life. True devotion to the heart of Jesus, he claimed, depended on the realization of human misery and the need for God's grace and mercy. His reflections attempt to combine a theological understanding of God with the prayerful cry of personal need, the infinitely great, all-encompassing power and grandeur of God with the personal love of Jesus.

Delp completed reflections on only five of the invocations. It is possible that after the fifth day he found himself face to face with Advent, the time in the Church year to which he felt particularly drawn. His pen—held in bound hands, working its way across small sheets of paper, perhaps on his knees or on the edge of his plank bed—made a turn toward the meaning of the Incarnation.

"Advent is the time for rousing. . . . The primary condition for a fruitful and rewarding Advent is renunciation, surrender."[2] Thus begins his series of meditations on Advent. He continues by using his own situation as both a starting point and an end point in meditating on the meaning of this liturgical season. Here he languishes, wrists tied, imprisoned in a cell with no keyhole. He walks three paces in one direction, three in the other. He is hungry, lonely, and full of fear in the face of sinister forces. And this is the fate of each human: imprisoned in one's own state of consciousness, tied to earth and to one's own puny world, with nowhere to expand. The way out, the way to freedom, is to surrender, to let oneself be shaken awake, to face life with absolute honesty, to seek God above all things. He refers to the figure of an angel that he received once as a gift. "Be of good cheer, the Lord is near," the inscription read. A bomb destroyed the angel and also killed the friend who gave it to him. And yet the paradox: angels do bring good tidings.

Again and again he returns to the word *surrender:* surrender in the knowledge that only God holds the key to the prison cell; only God can open the door; and when God chooses to open the door, then one must be prepared with a spirit open to be led, to be changed, to become oneself, like the angel, the bearer of good tidings. This is what God came to earth to do: to open the prison door and to transform the fettered wrists into a sacrament of freedom.

As Christmas approached, Delp continued his reflections: by entering history, God takes on the burdens of human life, and this means that God is there to help us bear ours. Life is not made easier, he writes, but we know then that we are carried through the desolate stretches on life's road. Delp was critical, as with other Catholic devotions, of the sentimentalizing of the Nativity scene, and his Christmas meditations reflect his insistence on a realistic context: the babe in the manger remains the God of the universe and our final judge. He contemplates the attitudes of those in the stable—Mary, Joseph, and the shepherds—and those liturgically connected with the feast—St. Stephen, St. John, the Holy Innocents, St. Thomas Becket. He notes those not in attendance at the manger—the powerful, the wealthy, the learned. And then there is an urgency as he rushes to conclude his Christmas meditation: he hears the echoing sound of the guard's footsteps along the passageway and at the same time he realizes that his paper supply has run out. Whoever reads these hurried pages, he writes in a final scrawled sentence, will have to draw the threads together for themselves.

These meditations were sent first to Luise Oestreicher (as his secretary she had become accustomed to his pen scratches), and then, perhaps as Delp realized they might be of help to others during the dark days of bomb attacks and arbitrary Nazi cruelty, he encouraged her to pass copies on to others.

With all this burst of creativity on him, the prisoner of cell 8/313, who officially had no paper and pen and no contact with the outside world, got into the routine of doing most of his writing during the night hours, when there was less chance of being detected by guards.

———

To Franz von Tattenbach, S.J., December 1, 1944

Dear Tatt, loyal friend and comrade,

Thanks a lot for all your goodness and faithfulness. I can only tell God again and again that he has to be good to you for all your kindness which, even in this isolation, is still obvious and having an effect.

Actually, it's sometimes a bitter realization feeling and knowing how much I'm in debt to people. In fact, I'm now recognizing the important things. . . . Don't trouble yourself, my friend; I know well how the matter stands and that from a natural point of view, the case is hopeless. And yet detachment belongs somehow to our way of life, and I have never understood this as well as I do now. All the same, I still have a lot of trust and confidence. During these nineteen weeks, life has become immensely complex and multidimensional. God and death and freedom and miracle and guidance and surrender and trust: these all belong naturally to it. In the past a lot was masked. . . .

God bless you. Today is First Friday. This has always been a special day for me.[3] It was on the Feast of the Sacred Heart that I received the "letter of sacrifice," which you already know about. Today was a good day. Even though in the end we're chained and locked up, the heart of the day is the Mass. We pray and trust and are not in the least bit modest about what we expect from God. In fact, Moltke, Fugger, and Pastor Gerstenmaier and I are making a second novena in preparation for December 8. Unite your prayer a bit with ours. All the best. God bless you and warm greetings.

Bullus

To Maria Delp, early December 1944

Dear Mother,

A big thank-you for your good wishes and greetings. I'm so sorry that I'm causing you such worry and distress. God knows what he wants of us, and so we don't want to say no.

Dear good Mother, just let me thank you with all my heart for the goodness and care and devotedness that you've always had for us. We're the kind of people who feel this and are well aware of it but for the most part are unable to say it. I know what I owe you. I have you to thank for everything in my life that's good and fine and right. We should really have talked together more often about these things. But when I return, this false life must be left in the past. When we see each other again, your big boy will take his mother in his arms and give her a hearty kiss, and then we'll thank God together—okay?

Give everyone my best wishes. By the time you get this note, the decision will likely have come down and we'll know my fate. Whichever way it goes, *Mutterle,* don't be angry at God. He has willed it for the best.

Let's pray for and with each other. My best wishes to everyone. And to you, lots of love and good wishes.

Alfred

To Luise Oestreicher, December 5, 1944

Dear L.,

I'm sorry that I begged you for a word of affirmation the other day. I actually wanted to know whether you still honestly believe that I'm going to be coming back. Sometimes I really need that because of my isolation. I still think I'll be released, but everything is against me. I've been earnestly warned to take death more seriously and not to underestimate the present situation. Good friends have written me that, and more.

I'm aware that I'm on a tightrope. I'm also aware that I'm not going to get across without God's special help and blessing. But I believe that God is going to help me and I tell him that every day.

Once again it's an open question when the trial is going to take place. Yesterday it looked as if it had been postponed until after Christmas. Today they're again saying that it might be as soon as next week. *Deus providebit* [God will provide]. Anyway, I now know what it's like to live from his hand. We should always live that way, but I've still sometimes put a lot of stock on my own resources and security. And as a result, I've been guilty of so much toward so many people. You're one of them. . . . So you'll find that I want to be a blessing for you, and I will be.

God bless you, and greetings to all our friends.

Georg

(Thanks for the relief you sent for my teeth. It's working very well.)

Don't worry. I'm already trying hard not to refuse God anything.

CHAPTER 9

COMPLETE
SURRENDER

December 8–December 31, 1944

Sometime before the end of the first week of December, Delp learned that the trial had been moved back to an unspecified date. By this time, however, he was already leading his friends in a novena leading up to the originally scheduled date, December 8, the Feast of the Immaculate Conception. His own intention in this series of prayers was that God might give him some assuring sign of continuing care.

On the morning of December 8, a guard arrived at Delp's cell with a note written on an official order form. The note was signed by Marianne Hapig. "Mr. Franz is coming in an hour to discuss a most important personal matter," the note read, in thinly veiled code. And then, "Max's vow day has been moved from August 15, 1944, to today." The note continued, "Our friend Franz has been promoted and in spite of his youth has full authority."[1] This was the news that Tattenbach was in Berlin and that Franz Xaver Müller (who had replaced Rösch as the Jesuit provincial superior after Rösch had gone into hiding) had given him the authority to receive Delp's final vows.

About an hour after Delp received this news, a guard unlocked his door, unshackled him, and led him to the main wing of the prison, where he was brought to the small meeting room. Tattenbach stood waiting; Delp sat down at the table. Tattenbach sat on his right and the guard on his left. They chatted for a brief while, Delp asking for news and Tattenbach relaying greetings from various people. The question of Delp's legal defense then came up, and Tattenbach produced the application form for Delp to fill out as a request for a new lawyer. At this point, they may have also discussed the possibility of using Delp's articles and his small book *Humanity and History* as means in his defense.

Finally, Tattenbach leaned across Delp and addressed the guard. There was one more brief matter to discuss, he said. It was simply a Latin text to be signed, he added, not of any significance as far as the trial was concerned. He produced a sheet of paper from his pocket and held it toward the guard. Would the guard care to look at it? Would he like to see a translation? The guard looked at the two of them with suspicion. He then glanced at the document and seeing that it was incomprehensible to him, waved it away. Tattenbach handed the sheet to Delp. Delp read the typed vow formula and then sank back in his chair. Tattenbach, concerned that his Jesuit brother might not want to take this decisive step in such extreme circumstances, pressed him to sign it. In a quick gesture, Delp sat up, took the pen, and holding it tightly, signed his name in a shaking scrawl.

Suddenly, Tattenbach, who had not yet made final vows himself, remembered that for the vows to be valid, the vow formula had to be read aloud. He pressed Delp to read it again, this time out loud. Delp picked up the sheet and began to read, his voice breaking: *"Ego Alfredus Delp professionem facio, et promitto omnipotenti*

Deo coram eius virgine Matre, et universa caelesti curia . . ." ("I, Alfred Delp, solemnly promise and swear to almighty God before his Virgin Mother and the whole heavenly court . . ."). He read the formula to the end, sobs punctuating the words. Tattenbach, taken aback by the depth of Delp's emotion, put on a distant, business-like air so as not to arouse the guard's suspicions further. He took the signed vows, stood up, and with little more talk, left.

Delp was led back to his cell and once again locked in. Outwardly, nothing particularly significant had taken place, but for Delp, his final vows marked a major spiritual turning point. He regarded them as outward proof that, no matter what happened to him, his life was formally in God's hands and that his act of sur-render was held forever within the folds of the community in which he had cast his lot nearly two decades earlier.

Perhaps it was this event that released further energies within him and allowed him to return in spirit to his life of intellectual probing and critical thinking. He began a series of discourses in which he returned to his previous themes on the state of Western society, which he claimed had become "Godless," and on the Church, which he considered to be in serious need of reform. Some of these discourses he wrote in the form of letters that he addressed "To M.," possibly referring to *Mitbrüder,* or "fellow Jesuits," but which probably included a wider circle of friends. Others he wrote in more general terms, under the title, "Reflections on the Future." As dated by the Mariannes, these discourses appear to have been begun at the end of December, but, in fact, Delp began writing them at least two weeks earlier. Like the meditations, these reflections found their way first to Luise Oestreicher, who received permission to visit Delp on December 15.

———

To Franz von Tattenbach, S.J., December 9, 1944

Dear T.,

Thanks so much, thank you, thank you. I'm sorry I got so emotional. It was so much at one time. And such an answer to prayer! All during the novena leading up to the 8th, I prayed for a message of mercy. And there it was. *Calculo mundasti ignito* [You have cleansed with a burning stone].[2] I hope that my lips were pure and my desire sincere and honest. I have handed over my life completely. The external chains mean nothing anymore, now that God has found me worthy of the *vincula amoris* [chains of love].[3] A shadow was cast when it seemed that God didn't want me to make my vows on August 15. He was only letting me prepare further.

Thank you for the help you're giving my family, etc. It's a big help to know this is going on, no matter what happens to me.

I knew that Dr. Wehrle was lost as soon as I heard why he was here. But of course that should never be made known.

To the matters at hand: I know very well that this is serious business. Still, I'm taking God seriously, very seriously, where he tells us that trust has power over him. It's sometimes exhausting to hold oneself in freedom and at the same time remain trusting.

As far as the Kreisau matters are concerned, we might be let off. I think the choice of the new lawyer is a positive move.

The most important thing for me is to get rid of Sperr's last statements, which are incorrect. The lawyer must try to bring Sperr himself to the trial, and not just his statements. The other charge from Cologne will be dropped if it's possible to bring that man. He's prepared to take a risk. He's also ready to write a letter, but for that I'm going to try first with Sperr. Having both would be too noticeable. Besides, Letterhaus spoke about the same conversation in a way that was helpful to me.

P.S. The rest of the day went very well. A little past noon I got hold of myself again. Do pray for me. I'm astonished and embarrassed that I was so emotional. That's the first time I let myself go like that. I'll have to be careful.

Mass in the evening was full of graces. Please pray the Introit in the same heartfelt spirit I had yesterday! And then, keeping in mind my situation, yesterday's evening prayer. I didn't sleep much last night. For a long time I sat before my tabernacle and just kept praying the Suscipe.[4] In all the variations that applied to me in this situation. Now and then during the late evening I read from the seventh book of the *Republic:* Plato's famous cave image . . . from shadows to reality.

I'd like the *formula subscripta*[5] kept safe from bombs. It would be too bad for all concerned if it got lost. I was supposed to write a letter saying I was leaving the Society of Jesus. This would be a great substitute.

Many thanks to all and best wishes. You're a good friend, Tatt. It's very good not just to know that, but to have heard and seen it. I've dealt with this whole tough situation so well since then. May God protect you.

Yours, A.

To Franz von Tattenbach, S.J., December 13, 1944

Dear T.,

Once again, thanks a lot for the multiple blessings you brought. Very gradually my new being is taking hold inside. And spreading through me in a warm and peaceful way. It's all providential. I was right at a critical point where I was suffering a lot from isolation. And sometimes heaven remains silent; I heard nothing from friends and saw nothing happening on the matter at hand. I prayed, literally, for something to lift my spirits on the 8th, and for a message of mercy. And see what happened!

I'm also glad that you've been looking after matters for me. It helps to know that someone better and more interested is involved. The lawyer hasn't yet been allowed to speak with me. Yesterday he was here for the second time and so I let it be known I'd like to talk with him. He came by for a short time and said that he still didn't have permission but was applying for it. So should something be done to help get it?

By the way, reporting on the bomb damage is a good enough reason for a visit. There must still be a lot of rubbish lying around.

Greetings to our friends: Fix, Joseph Blumenau, Max Bernauer, Knigge, etc. I'm not forgetting Laplace, Dominique, and Secchi. All the best. Now it's feeling more like Advent—I'm looking forward to Monday evening.

May God bless you and reward you for everything.

Bullus

To Luise Oestreicher, week ending December 15, 1944

Dear L.,

I hear you've been sick. In that case, please don't come here. I know well how it is with you. Your heart is already too burdened with worry and distress and now once again you're pushed to the limit of what you can take, or perhaps you've even gone past that limit. Unfortunately, I can help you only on another level.

In spite of everything, I wish you a blessed Christmas. To you has been given a profound, joyful meeting with the mystery of light which overcomes the night. We always have to begin everything again from the inside.

Tonight I read through a large part of the Gospel at one go. One never finishes reading this book. The urgency, uniqueness and victorious qualities of God's character always find a new way to touch and wake up the soul to enlightenment, belief, and discipleship. And the call to faith and trust is still there on each page. Tonight was truly beautiful, and I firmly believe now that God is going to bring me across the tightrope.

It seems now that the trial will be next week (the 19th and 20th). I still don't know how I'm going to find an escape hatch. *Deus providebit* [God will provide]. Do you have news of Gusti? Please, take decent care of yourself. Greetings to your family and to my friends.

God protect you. Thank you and good-bye.

Georg

To Maria Delp, beginning of December 1944

Dear Mother,

Many thanks for your greetings and your dear words. Please don't tire yourself out, *Mutterl*. For certain, God makes everything right. Pray and hope—hope and pray. I hope all of you in Munich came through all right. I'm glad you're being well looked after. And you'll like it out in the countryside as well. Greetings to the teachers and to everyone in Wolferkam. I'm doing fine. I think I'm going to celebrate a truly beautiful Christmas. Alone with God. Is Greta in Munich already? Take good care of Marianne, and don't spoil her—now please remember! And keep up your courage, dear Mother. God isn't going to let us down. Everything's going to turn out just fine, you'll see, and you'll get your three boys back again. May the Christ child bring much joy to your heart.

Your big troublemaker

To Luise Oestreicher, December 16, 1944

Dear L.,

What a gift it was to see you. Let's both be really brave, okay? It's strange how a person can live a double life, saying one thing, knowing another and feeling another. I had a faint hope today that you might bring an Advent light under the heading "coat." But you'll probably have been on your way back already.

You don't look well at all. But of course why should you? If all your friendships are as totally exhausting as your friendship with me, then it's no wonder.

I hope it will be possible to get the Advent meditation out tomorrow. That will be some feast-day deciphering for you. . . .

I spoke with my lawyer today. This is the way it is: my head lies in the Donaustrasse.[6] If nothing starts flowing from there, then there's just nothing to be done. So we'll just have to pray for a miracle there as well. Will you keep on helping me? . . . It's so good to have seen a good person once again. I just wish I could have been able to unload some of your worries.

Please make sure that someone in Ecking looks out for Marianne—perhaps the school principal or Annaliese or Mandi.

God bless you, and a blessed Christmas. Help me to hold on, or else I'll be torn to pieces again. And then everything will be as hopeless as it was on the first day. Help me to pray that all the locks break. And pray with me, that I get across. I've been feeling today as though I simply had to run away. And now the handcuff guy is coming. God bless you.

Georg

Things are okay again. For Christmas, beg God for the Donaustrasse to fall through for me. The man has to write a letter. Perhaps, if they allow it, I'll need a typist for a few days after Christmas.

I've been feeling in every fiber of my being the realization that you were here in August.

To Luise Oestreicher, December 16, 1944[7]

Dear L.,

I don't know whether or not this is a farewell letter. These days we just never know. I don't know if or when these lines will ever reach you, but I'm not writing them as a "last word." In some part of myself, I believe with a firm certainty in life and in a new mission. But I'm also honest enough to say that from a human point of view, I don't see much possibility of that. . . .

How am I doing? There's not much to say. If the Donaustrasse sticks to his statement, I'm dead. If he's sensible and reasonable enough to revise it, perhaps the matter can be straightened out orally. Perhaps. As far as official records are concerned, I've been written off.

What used to be called elegance and self-confidence has all been completely and utterly crushed. Painfully. Don't worry—I'm going to try hard not to break down, even if I have to go to the gallows. I know that God's strength is with me the whole way. But it's sometimes really quite tough. There have been moments when Georg is nothing more than a bloody whimper. (It's now evening. We're not able to write much these days because most of the time, day and night, we're handcuffed.) But Georg is always trying to transform these whimpers into the only two realities that make this place worthwhile: adoration and love. Everything else is false. Believe me, these weeks have been a kind of bitter and unrelenting judgment on my past life. In fact, it isn't past. It's standing right here as a big question demanding its final answer, its seal. If I may once still . . .

Yes—if and whether I still can! God has now put me in a place where I can't get out. And whatever I've undertaken has failed. One door after another has closed. Even the ones I thought were open for good. No help has come from the outside, and probably couldn't anyway. About what happens inside it's better to be silent. So here I've been put now, handcuffed and locked in a narrow cell. There are only two ways out: one is through the gallows into the light of God, and the other through a miracle into a new mission. Which way do I think I'll be going, here in the "kindergarten of death"? We're taken outside for an hour and in a bullheaded manner are led around in a circle, closely watched, with guns, etc. All the other people around are shooed away. So then we walk around in the circle, handcuffed, counts and civil servants, officers and laborers, diplomats and economists. At some corners you can speak toward the wall and the person behind hears you. That's how conversations take place in the "kindergarten of death." Yesterday I asked a Protestant friend whether we were still having a church service. "Of course," he replied. "I'd rather hope myself to death than perish in unbelief."

During these weeks I've learned and relearned enough for years. . . .[8]

To Franz Sperr, December 16, 1944

Sperr:

Since after all we're now going to be tried separately—and by the way, the reading of your evidence is likely enough to finish me—I beg you to make a change in your statement immediately in a letter to the president of the People's Court, with a copy to Fr. Delp's assigned counsel at the People's Court. This letter is important and must arrive soon, because the president makes his judgment at home when he reads the files and changes nothing after that. Besides, there won't be a chance of making a change orally in the present state of affairs. Please notify me somehow so that I know where I stand on this matter. Right now I'm working out a way of writing it to show support for you. Moltke has written one as well, in an effort to help you. Please send an answer.

To Franz von Tattenbach, S.J., December 16, 1944

Dear Tatt,

Many thanks for your goodness and care. Luise was here yesterday and I was on "better behavior" than I was with you. Also, it wasn't as shocking and exciting as the confirmation you brought of my inner existence. The lawyer was here today. (He told me, not without a greedy sidelong glance, about the *captatio benevolentiae* [sympathetic consideration] you brought him. It's important that he be given a few things. We obviously can't expect that much is going to happen for the 80 RM [reichsmark] that the state is paying him for my head. Is it possible to step up his enthusiasm? He told me yesterday that he's not allowed to take *money*. By the way, he defended Dr. Wehrle. It seems the two of them stirred each other up.)

The situation is just as I knew it to be: if Sperr's statement remains, I'll fall because of this one sentence. If it's not used, there's a chance since all the rest has to do with Kreisau matters, some of it silly stuff. The Cologne incrimination will sort itself out, since the man will probably be tried with me and has promised to do an about-face.

Now somebody here has to take on the systematic task of contacting Sperr. Over where he is there are a lot of ways of doing it. Someone just has to get going on it. The trial's delay is truly a great grace and help. Sperr must right now give evidence in writing; since we'll probably be tried separately, I'll only be questioned with the others. Besides, Freisler makes his judgment when he reads the files and never changes it during the proceeding.

Greetings to all. Thanks a lot. I hope you'll never need to experience how consoling it is when someone is looking after you. Moltke has submitted a good statement for the defense. The people in the Reich's security headquarters are shaking their heads over it. A good Advent light—

Georg

Do you know anyone I spoke to about my visit with Stauffenberg? Lord, to hang for such a piece of nonsense.

Also, we have to find out whether certain people have been arrested or not. From the point of view of the charge, the three-week delay is probably our salvation. Otherwise, I would have needed someone outside who had time. As well, the lawyer must have access to certain files. I need the books to make some statements. That means he's going to have to come back. Do you have much time?

Article and book here, and point out to the lawyer the places where the charge is contradicted. Replace arguments by "general opinion."

———

To Franz von Tattenbach, S.J., December 18, 1944

Dear T.,

Thank you. It's reassuring to know of your goodness and loyalty. That way, at least I know that everything possible is being done, and nothing is left undone. Please send me news soon of how Munich is doing after yesterday's attack. My mother and the little girl are still there.

The charge against me is unbelievable. Even the points that are correct are full of spite and misleading vagueness and confusion. Here are the incriminating points:

1. A distorted description of Kreisau, which makes this high treason in itself.
2. Sperr's statement—absolutely deadly.
3. Gross's statement about Cologne—Goerdeler as well as Moltke wanted to stage a coup, according to a statement I'm supposed to have made.
4. Moltke and I apparently gave each other information about Goerdeler's plans for a coup.

5. I had apparently recommended Reisert to Moltke as
   provincial commissioner.

6. I supposedly took part in a meeting where it was
   discussed that a group of officers wanted a coup.

Point 1: Let's hope we can correct this by agreeing on the most important points.

The lawyers think it's going to fall between the cracks. The fatal part is the connection with July 20.

Point 2: Here is the real catch. It must be loosened. But how? Please keep going after him, systematically. The best course would be for him to write a letter taking back what he'd said earlier, "after thinking about it," etc. Or move that statement onto König. I can't understand how the man got this idea. Perhaps it's also still possible to get help from the following people:

Georg Wessling: He knew that I was going to see Stauffenberg, because he asked me if I knew anyone who could do something for Emil Piepke, who was arrested here in Berlin. I suspect that Georg's arrest was connected with that matter. So he doesn't need to be afraid of that anymore. After July 20 he came to me full of concern and asked me whether I was worried and didn't I want to leave? I told him that I didn't see any reason, since I'd known nothing about the matter and had had nothing to do with it.

Ernst Ismaninger: Same thing. He often asked me whether I was worried. I gave him the same answer. That would at least help to support my case—from this fact, one could point out that I felt safe and wasn't burdened by knowing anything beforehand.

Our conversation that morning could likely be interpreted in a similar fashion. I just told the Gestapo here that the first news I got of the Führer's address was from a workman, because I didn't want to indicate that you'd come here so early. When the Gestapo said that you'd been arrested, I told them that you were with me that morning and had upbraided me for bringing your family into this area. I'd said that I was duped as well and knew as little as you did and had explained that to your family.

This Sperr problem has to get cleared up. But how?

Point 3: This will be all right if we succeed in getting Gross as a witness. It looks fine. We also have to get the suppressed interrogations of Letterhaus and Müller here. On this point I absolutely have to know, and soon, whether Siemer O.P. and Kaiser have been arrested. The position with the whole Goerdeler case has been improved by the fact that Moltke had warned us that Goerdeler was a Gestapo spy story. The Gestapo knew about all this and could prove it.

Point 4: This is finally put to rest with no. 3. Moltke had not said anything.

Point 5: This is incorrect. Moltke will challenge it.

Point 6: Since I didn't participate in any Berlin meeting without Moltke, this can be corrected.

Because in the end everything is simply based on my views, I'll have to point out what I've written. I must get my articles "Christ and the Present Time," "War As a Spiritual Achievement," "People," "Homeland," and the little book, to give the lawyer a sampling to taste.

But the lawyer wants on his next visit to check out the statements on which the separate incriminations are based. Perhaps Steltzer still has to be suitably asked about things.

Is it possible for him to get me a typewriter for one or two days? I want to type up something for him. With my handwriting it's catastrophic. Regardless of that, I'm requesting a package of paper that I can write on in ink, with lines as narrow as possible. Then I'll set out with my scribble.

What is life all about? In here it seems quite weird. Everything so hopeless, and yet while acknowledging the gravity of the situation, we don't feel lost. Together, the four of us have again started a novena for Christmas. Praying the *Una Sancta in vinculis* [One Holy in chains]. Every day Mass is said for Moltke in the crypt of St. Gereon in Cologne. I say it here, Stöttner in Munich. Oh, if only the star of Christmas would finally rise. Trying to communicate takes up a lot of time because of the isolation.

All the best. God reward you, and I end this with a blessing.

Georg

Luise still has copies of the little book. I'd also like to give one to [. . .] and to the two Mariannes, whose copies got burnt. . . .

It's also important to find out whether Gross will be tried with me, as was originally thought, and how my trial is linked to the others.

Some ink please. Mine is just about finished.

———

To [Unknown], December 1944[9]

You are one of the few people I feel here with me and to whom I remain grateful, as I stand here now at the edge, where I've left behind so much of what seemed indispensable and necessary.

I'd just like to express my deepest gratitude to you and ask you to pray for me, no matter what happens. It requires a lot of strength, living like this between the gallows and a miracle.

I always was a strange kid. In fact, I remained a kid and have finally started to become a man before God and for God. And now it's all happening in a rush. I hope that God is counting these sixteen weeks because of the burden they've brought, over and over again, and the strength they've required.

How are things going to go? I don't know. And I don't know why. It's gradually coming closer. There aren't many of us left. God bless you, thank-you, and greetings to everyone.

Gratefully,

Delp

I've sent Frau Oestreicher, who will get this note, a few written thoughts on the Church, the Society, etc. And also an update on my situation. Don't let up on the prayers. Most of the time God still has a way out the back door.

Greetings to Tattenbach.

To Franz von Tattenbach, S.J., after December 18, 1944

Consider this: wouldn't it be possible, from our conversation of July 21, to give testimony to the effect that I had no suspicion either of Stauffenberg's plans or of Sperr's knowledge? As far as I know, I even told you then that I wanted to make inquiries as to whether Sperr knew anything.

Consider whether it's a good idea for you to put yourself into this risky area. Then discuss with the lawyer the possibilities that remain for making an exonerating statement. In that case I'd have to be told exactly what you say so that I can recount the conversation in the same way.

Because Rösch and König have disappeared, there's naturally great suspicion that we knew about July 20. What a fix. But it's the fact that Sperr's statement was wrong that reveals the whole thing to be God's providence and test.

Try and see again if it's possible to make contact with Sperr. The Mariannes will already have given you information.

Greetings and thanks to everyone. It was a day of great mercy today. Thanks and God bless you.

B.

You'll have heard the rumor that I've left the Society. That's one reason I've been put into isolation. It's not correct. The only thing that's correct is that I said I didn't understand why Rösch had disappeared. We've openly defended Kreisau; we've explained everything—that we didn't want to cause anyone's downfall, but wanted only to keep something alive. Then the objection always came back: Then why have Rösch and König disappeared? They learned a few very stupid things about König. Luckily that was after I'd been given the beatings, when I'd already arrived here. If I should be sentenced to death, the time between the sentence and the execution is, in a way, mercifully short. *Deus providebit.* Keep praying and having faith.

Bullus

To Luise Oestreicher, December 22, 1944

Dear L.,

I wish I could have an hour with you. Not for my sake. I think my Christmas will be a joyful one. But to be with you and to help you discover some of the Christmas spirit. I send you my blessing, and I ask the Christ child, the world's great Mystery, to be with you.

Once again you've been through bitter hours and days in Munich. I haven't yet had news about how you are. From the newspaper it seems that the disaster hit in your area, and was especially close to you yourself. Please send news soon.

Right now it's a matter of waiting and holding on. I have prayed mightily to God for a Christmas light. Perhaps he'll send one of his special graces again. He has so many means of helping us get up and keeping us going. So often have I felt this during these long and anxious weeks.

I have increased confidence. It's consoling to know I have the prayer and loyalty of friends with me. These are the important realities. God versus worldly power; God is with us in fidelity, love, and confidence.

I'd like to light some candles for you. You have been with me in my night, and you still have your own darkness to live through. We are all in this together, for sure. Together we'll pull through. And in the midst of night, the light will shine. You'll see. Let's help one another, not wearily, but singing and praying the old carols and prayers, more earnestly and soberly than before, but in a way that is closer to reality.

Christmas greetings to your family. Is there news of Gusti? Greetings to Annemarie and the whole group. All the best to everyone. Good-bye.

The brother of one of the Mariannes was acquitted![10]

Georg

———

To Marianne Hapig and Marianne Pünder, December 22, 1944

Good people! There's just enough time to write an ordinary note because I don't know when the man is coming back with the handcuffs. I wanted to write a decent letter, but after all, what is decent these days? I'm really happy about the Christmas gift God has given you. Ever since I was aware of this worry, I've been keeping the mountain in place with you, lest it topple over in an avalanche. You should have told me about it a lot earlier.[11] God is good—we certainly discover that fact all the time.

I'm still saying Monday's Mass for you. Do whatever you want with it. I'm so glad to have this opportunity to thank you at least a little bit.

It looks like the trial date is not going to be before January 15. But it's still not certain.

And now we're going to be celebrating Christmas. And it's going to be a beautiful Christmas, despite everything, or perhaps because of everything. With the stage setting gone these days, it's real, without obstruction, and a person can stand and face ultimate reality. The lightning that has struck us has also burned away our romantic concepts. But that's how it should always be. A Father of the Church calls Christmas the mystery of the great howl, because the creature is completely shaken by the manner in which God takes a stand with the human race. Since our utterly bourgeois respectability prevents us from being capable of this howl any more, God has for the time being once again taught us what a shaking—a shaking, shaken world—means! I think that from all of this we're going to have a watchful and blessed time with the

Child. The contradiction of everything we take for granted, the setting aside of all our important matters. Powerlessness on the tightrope is an education in understanding the Child. When I've understood it enough, then I can come down.

God reward you for everything. And please don't give up on prayer and confidence. My new virtue is indefatigability.

May God protect all of you.

Max

To Luise Oestreicher, end of December 1944

Dear L.,

Christmas was lovely and peaceful. I felt your help close to me. Sometime the Advent that began last summer will find its light, its fulfillment, and its return home. I had actually dreaded these days, but they were peaceful and blessed. My Mass at night was my most beautiful Christmas Mass ever. I was actually able to get away from my worrisome situation. And for a short while I even allowed myself to dream about what it would be like to be back in Munich soon. I visited my mother as well as you and my other friends. All the best for the new year. God's protection and blessing. And in spite of everything, much more blessing, success, courage, strength, and joy in your heart. Good-bye.

Georg

Please: a copy of the little book to Professor Wiese, Karlshorst, Guntherstrasse 6. And thanks for taking good care of the books. God's protection on everyone in 1945.

To M., December 28, 1944

In the course of these last long weeks, life has become suddenly much less rigid. A great deal that was once quite simple and ordinary seems to have taken on a new dimension. Things seem clearer and at the same time more profound; one sees all sorts of unexpected angles. And above all, God has become almost tangible. Things I have always known and believed now seem so concrete; I believe them, but I also live them.

For instance, how I used to mouth the words *hope* and *trust*. I know now that I used them uncomprehending, like a child. And in doing so I deprived my life of much fruitfulness and achievement and I also cheated my fellow human beings of many substantial blessings because I was incapable of taking really seriously God's command that we should trust him absolutely and wholeheartedly. Only someone who really believes and hopes and trusts can form any idea of humanity's real status or catch a glimpse of the divine perspective.

To M., December 29, 1944

Far more than a civilization or a rich heritage was lost when the universal order went the way of medieval and ancient civilizations. Western humanity today is spiritually homeless, naked, and exposed. The moment we start to be anything beyond "one of the masses" we become terribly aware of that isolation which has always encompassed the great. We realize our homelessness and exposure. So we set to work to build ourselves some sort of house and shelter. Our ancestors, those among them who were really great, could have left us a legacy much more helpful for our progress. We can only account for the contorted thought of people like Paracelsus[12] or Böhme[13] on the grounds that life's insufferable loneliness and lack of design forced them to build a shelter for themselves. And although it is such a self-willed and distorted and angular structure, it still has the marks of painstaking care and trouble and in that must command our respect. Goethe had rather more success; his instinct was surer and it led him to guess at some of nature's more important designs. Moreover, he had a good—though not in all respects dependable—master whose ideas he copied to a very large extent.

Every now and then someone comes along and tries to impose his own plan on the rest of the world, either because he knows he has stumbled on a universal need or because he thinks he has and overestimates his own infallibility. Such people will never lack followers since there are so many who long for a well-founded communal home to which they can feel they "belong." Time after time in the end they come to realize that the shelter offered is not all it purports to be—it cannot keep out the wind and the weather. And time and time again the deluded seekers conclude they have been taken in by a mountebank who probably had no intention of deliberately deceiving but was nevertheless a charlatan misleading himself and others. . . .

It is quite remarkable. Since Midnight Mass on Christmas Eve I have become almost lightheartedly confident although nothing outwardly has changed. Somewhere within me ice has been melted by the prayers for love and life—I cannot tell on what plane. There is nothing tangible to show for it and yet I am in good heart and my thoughts soar. Of course the pendulum will swing back and there will be other moods—the sort that made St. Peter tremble at the wind and the waves.

I have a great yearning to talk to a few well-loved friends. When?

To M., December 30, 1944

Everything is still in the balance. Yesterday news filtered through by the grapevine that Bolz has been condemned.[14] No one knows whether sentence has already been carried out or not. . . .

For endurance one has to rely on resources outside oneself. I find three great supports: *fiat misericordia tua* [show forth your mercy]; *quemadmodum speravimus* [we have trusted in you]; *in patientia possidebitis animas vestras* [in patience you shall possess your souls]. Steadfastness really is a virtue; it is not merely temperament. . . .

To Franz von Tattenbach, S.J., December 31, 1944

Dear Tatt,

Wishing you all the best, and may God protect you in the coming new year. Who knows what it's going to bring? The Father's will in its ever-changing forms, or in its ultimate form? *Fiat* [Let it be done].

I'm relatively okay. Christmas brought a beautiful peace that is still with me. As a result, I'm optimistic and confident.

Physically, I'm plagued with a mild case of the flu at the moment. Not bad, just stupid, because one always feels so stupid with it. The Mariannes' various pills are working well.

To business: Keep after Sperr. . . . Consider what you think about the possibilities. I really don't think the guy, as confused as he is, is capable of making an about-turn in a public trial.

I'm going to spend this last day of the year mostly on my personal concerns. I still have Mass to look forward to, and I also intend to gather up the whole year in one prayer and one act of surrender. There are really only a few true words that the human spirit is capable of.

All the best, and may God protect you. I hope I'll never have to repay you in this particular form of loyalty and care. But I'll gladly do it in any other form. May God reward you. *In nomine Domini* [In the name of the Lord].

Georg

―――――

To Eugen Gerstenmaier, December 31, 1944

Dear Gerstenmaier,

. . . That was a beautiful Christmas gift. And when we're out of here again let's show that it meant and still means more than a personal relationship. We'll have to keep on carrying as a burden and a legacy the historical weight of the separated Churches. But it should never again become a Christian disgrace. I have as little faith as you have in utopian mixtures, but still, the one Christ is undivided and wherever undivided love leads to him, there we will accomplish much more than our quarreling ancestors and contemporaries. Besides Mass, I also have the Sacrament at all times in my cell, and I speak to the Lord often about you. He's consecrating us here for a new mission. All the best, and may you have his gracious protection.

Yours, Delp

To M., December 31, 1944

The experience we are all passing through must surely at least produce one thing—a passionate love of God and desire for his glory. As far as I am concerned, I find I have to approach him in a new and quite personal way. I must remove all the barriers that still stand between him and me, I must break down all the hidden reserve that keeps me from him. The prayer of van der Flue must become a living reality.[15] Divine life within me as faith, hope, and love. All this must combine with my temperament, abilities, faults, limitations, together with external circumstance to form a new mission, a pattern to whose realization I am now pledged.

In a quiet hour tonight I will pass in review the year now ending, recollecting my personal acts in a prayer of repentance, of gratitude, of resignation, in short of trust and love.

I have to keep reminding myself what is happening and wonder whether I am suffering from hallucinations or self-deception. There can be no overstating the seriousness of the situation and yet it all seems like a bad dream, quite unreal. Our Lord himself demanded that we should have the kind of faith that moves mountains, the trust that never fails. To him these were part of an infallible law that we can and must take seriously. Apart from the occasion when he drove the merchant from the temple, we know of only one occasion on which he was really angry and that was when the apostles failed to heal the boy sick with the palsy because they had no confidence in their power. Surely we can remove by faith and prayer the one obstacle on which all this mistrust rests. When I think of the grace and the guidance vouchsafed to me in the past in spite of all that I have done . . .

To M., New Year's Night, 1944–1945

It is difficult to sum up the year now ending in a few words. So much has happened during this year, and yet I cannot see what its real message is for me, or its real achievement. Generally speaking, it has not produced anything really effective. Hardship and hunger and violence have intensified and are all now more shattering than anyone could have imagined. The world lies in ruins around us. It is full of hatred and enmity. Everyone clings to their few miserable possessions because these are the last remaining things that they can really call their own.

Spiritually, we seem to be in an enormous vacuum. Humanly speaking there is the same burning question—what is the point of it all? And in the end even that question sticks in one's throat. Scarcely anyone can see, or even guess at, the connection between the corpse-strewn battlefields, the heaps of rubble we live in, and the collapse of the spiritual cosmos of our views and principles, the tattered residue of our moral and religious convictions as revealed by our behavior. And even if the connection were fully understood, it would be only a matter for academic interest, data to be noted and listed. No one would be shocked or deduce from the facts a need for reformation. We have already traveled so far in our progress toward anarchy and nihilism. Luckily, powerful interests still oppose the hordes from across the steppes, for the world could not survive an alliance with them.

How can one assess the nations of today? Portugal is in a kind of sleeping beauty trance—foreigners will eventually decide her future. Spain will go into the melting pot again because she did not meet her last challenge squarely but solved the problem by cheating. Nowadays there is no room for feudalism even when it masquerades as people's tribunals. The only solutions are social ones. Spain has missed her chance to her eternal shame—and the shame of the Church, too, who stood by and made no protest. Italy has become purely objective. The transition from historical subject to historical object has hardly ever been made more quickly. Past guilt and ruptured loyalties make her suspect as a friend; no ally trusts her—quite apart from her people's inability to make history and the country's lack of historical genius from the modern point of view. Nothing was ever achieved in Italy without war and violence—and after all, all that's left is a few fine rather strained attitudes. Poland is paying a bitter penalty for her conceited pretensions and offenses against other nations, particularly in the East. The Poles have never had much sense of reality though individually they are fine people. The Balkans lie at present in Russia's shadow. If as a result of all this suffering they should be at last welded into unity that would at least be one gain. For Hungary, I fear a severer judgment. Many mistakes have been made there, particularly social ones. The Scandinavians are just waiting to see who will take them or force them to submit to foreign influence.

Russia is inscrutable. One really ought to visit Russia. Communism is nothing more than a donkey for an imperialism of limitless proportions. When Russia dreams, she dreams magnificently and her fantasies are of unparalleled splendor.

Possibly, Communism needs the balance provided by Russia's interests. In any case, a Russian-dominated Europe could not last long. Russia still has a great deal to learn—she is too undisciplined herself to rule others. The Slavs have not yet been absorbed by the West and are like a foreign body in the working of the machine. They can destroy and annihilate and carry away enormous quantities of booty, but they cannot yet lead or build up. France is as disunited as ever, the moment Western tension relaxes. Unless she joins hands with Germany she will go the way of Russia and fly to extremes. That England is on the down grade even I am beginning to believe. The English have lost their keenness and their spiritual gifts; the philosophy of materialism has eaten into England's bones and paralyzed the muscles of her heart. The English still have great traditions and imposing forms and gestures; but what kind of people are they? The social problem has been overlooked in England—and also the problem of youth and the problem of America and of spiritual questions which can all too easily masquerade as cultural or political questions.

Germany on every plane is still struggling for its very existence. One thing is certain—there can be no Europe without Germany. And a Germany in which the original currents—Christianity, Germanism (not Teutonism) and classicism—no longer flow is not Germany at all and can be no help to the West. But here, quite apart from the outcome of the war, the more vital problem of bare subsistence plays a profoundly important part. In other words, our problem too is a social one.

The picture of the West for the moment is decidedly grim. Foreign and arbitrary powers—Russia and America—are thrusting irresponsible hands into our lives from all directions.

Finally, there are the Vatican and the Church to be considered. So far as concrete and visible influence goes, the attitude of the

Vatican is not what it was. It is not merely that it seems so because we get no information. Of course it will be shown eventually that the pope did his duty and more, that he offered peace, that he explored all possibilities to bring about peace negotiations, that he proclaimed the spiritual conditions on which a just peace could be based, that he dispensed alms and was tireless in his work on behalf of prisoners of war, displaced persons, tracing missing relatives and so on—all this we know and posterity will have documentary evidence in plenty to show the full extent of the papal effort. But to a large extent, all this good work may be taken for granted and also to a large extent it leads nowhere and has no real hope of achieving anything. That is the real root of the trouble—among all the protagonists in the tragic drama of the modern world there is not one who fundamentally cares in the least what the Church says or does. We overrated the Church's political machine and let it run on long after its essential driving power had ceased to function. It makes absolutely no difference so far [as] the beneficial influence of the Church is concerned whether a state maintains diplomatic relations with the Vatican or not. The only thing that really matters is the inherent power of the Church as a religious force in the countries concerned.

This is where the mistake started; religion died, from various diseases, and humanity died with it. Or perhaps it is truer to say that humanity died of great possessions, of modern development, of the pace of modern life and so on—and religion died as humanity succumbed. In any case, the West became a void so far as religion, as humanity and its spirit are concerned. In these circumstances, how can any word or act on the part of the Church awaken the slightest echo in world affairs? The Church faces the same tasks that nations and states and the Western world in general have to face—the problem of humanity, how people are to be housed and fed and how they can be employed in order to support themselves. In other words, we need social and economic regeneration. And then human beings also must be made aware of their true nature—in other words we need intellectual and religious regeneration. These are problems for the world, for individual states and nations, and they are also problems for the Church—far more so, for instance, than the question of liturgical forms. If these problems are solved without us, or to our disadvantage, then the whole of Europe will be lost to the Church, even if every altar faces the people and Gregorian chant is the rule in every parish. The supernatural demands a certain amount of expert action in regard to daily life, a degree of natural capacity for living without which life cannot survive. And the Church as an institution, an authority, requires a minimum of religious practice. Otherwise it can only have an idealistic value.

Therefore this year now ending leaves behind it a rich legacy of tasks and we must seriously consider how to tackle them. Above all else one thing is necessary—religious-minded people must become more devout; their dedication must be extended and intensified.

And that brings me to my own affairs. Have I grown in stature in the past year? Have I increased my value to the community? How do things stand with me?

Outwardly they have never been worse. This is the first New Year I have ever approached without so much as a crust of bread to my name. I have absolutely nothing I can call my own. The only gesture of goodwill I have encountered is that the guard has fastened my handcuffs so loosely that I can slip my left hand out entirely. The handcuffs hang from my right wrist so at least I am able to write. But I have to keep alert with one ear as it were glued to the door—heaven help me if they should catch me at work!

And undeniably I find myself in the very shadow of the scaffold. Unless I can disprove the accusations on every point I shall most certainly hang. The chances of this happening have never really seriously occupied my thoughts for long although naturally there have been moments of deep depression—handcuffs after all are a symbol of candidature for execution. I am in the power of the law which, in times like the present, is not a thing to be taken lightly.

An honest examination of conscience reveals much vanity, arrogance, and self-esteem; and in the past also a certain amount of dishonesty. That was brought home to me when they called me a liar while I was being beaten up. They accused me of lying when they found I mentioned no names except those I knew they knew already. I prayed hard, asking God why he permitted me to be so brutally handled and then I saw that there was in my nature a tendency to pretend and deceive.

On this altar much has been consumed by fire and much has been melted and become pliable. It has been one of God's blessings, and one of the signs of his indwelling grace, that I have been so wonderfully helped in keeping my vows. He will, I am confident, extend his blessing to my outward existence as soon as I am ready for the next task with which he wishes to entrust me. From this outward activity and intensified inner light, new passion will be born to give witness for the living God, for I have truly learned to know him in these days of trial and to feel his healing presence. *Dios solo basta* [God alone suffices] is literally and absolutely true.[16] And I must have a passionate belief in my mission to humanity, showing the way to a fuller life and encouraging the willing capacity for it. These things I will do wholeheartedly—*in nomine Domini.*

CHAPTER 10

INTO THE FIRE

January 1–January 8, 1945

As the new year of 1945 dawned, the war that resisters expected to be over two years earlier still raged, but it was now clear to nearly everyone that defeat was certain. Was it a question, though, of days, weeks, or months? The Allies were closing in on all sides, and Russian troops were said to be nearing Berlin. The country lay in ruins, yet air attacks were still finding new targets. The air-raid sirens wailed through the cold January air at least once every day now, and Berliners jostled and packed themselves together for hours in makeshift shelters. The city was an unrecognizable heap of rubble and smoldering shells of buildings. Food was in short supply, and an acute fuel shortage meant that hardship would only intensify as the harsh winter settled in.

Like others dedicated to prisoners who were friends or family members, the two Mariannes still made their way with clean laundry and other supplies through frozen, ghostly streets. Marianne Hapig's brother, Bernhard, who was a medical doctor as well as the provincial superior of the Jesuits' East German province, tended to air-raid victims. By now, nearly every family had been touched by death at least once as a result of the war. The supply of soldiers had been exhausted, and fourteen- and fifteen-year-olds were now being recruited from among the Hitler Youth. And yet anyone who mentioned that Germany might be defeated still ran the risk of arrest and execution.

The prisoner in cell 8/313 at Tegel Prison entered 1945 in an even worse physical state than he was used to. A skeleton staff of prison workers over the Christmas period meant that Delp was left alone with his hands tightly tied for longer periods than was normally the case. The Mariannes too went away for a few days, an absence that left him bereft of communication. And a mild case of the flu dragged him down and dulled his mind.

With every exploding bomb, he worried about the fates of his friends and family, particularly those in Munich. Unexpected visits from his sister Greta on January 2 and January 5 brought him a sense of welcome family warmth. Then the Mariannes brought the sad news that Luise Oestreicher's brother Gusti and Franz von Tattenbach's sister Luisette had been killed in bomb attacks. Anxiety continued on all sides: the head guard's son was sick; could the Mariannes come up with some help for the child? One wonders, in light of such a request, whether he fully realized the extent of the superhuman mission the two women were carrying out as the city crumbled around them.

Delp's Christmas Masses, however, had brought him a new peace, a deeper understanding of his reliance on God, a realization that imprisonment and powerlessness had changed him profoundly. Prayers of gratitude leaped out of him. He approached the Jesuits' special feast day, the Feast of the Holy Name, with childlike excitement.

On January 6, Delp began writing a meditation on the Epiphany. He again drew parallels between the Gospel story, his own life, and humanity as a whole. Like the Magi, he writes, he too has had to cross a wilderness, with a capricious, threatened ruler in the background who will go to any length to preserve his own power. And ahead, where one least expects to find it, is the encounter with God, and with this encounter, the moment of freedom. The guiding star cannot always be seen; when it is absent, there is confusion and doubt, and he is left wandering in the wilderness. This is the Epiphany image that remains foremost for Delp. The step into true freedom in every human life can be taken only by walking across whatever wilderness life presents, pushing the boundaries of personal limitations in a spirit of surrender. For him personally, he writes, it is a matter of leaving himself behind, of losing himself in God.

The words and themes in this meditation show how completely Delp had allowed himself to be stripped, how deeply he had become aware and accepting of his own misery and helplessness, how ready he was to become a seed planted in the earth and to let go of desire to see the fruit of his struggle. In handing the whole mess over to God, he seemed by now to have become a living embodiment of the prayer of St. Ignatius: "Take, O Lord, and receive my entire liberty, my memory, my understanding, and my whole will. All that I am and all that I possess you have given me: I surrender it all to you to be disposed of according to your will. Give me only your love and your grace; with these I will be rich enough, and will desire nothing more."

And yet he still longed for the prison door to open, to walk into the sunshine unshackled, to head back to Munich and St. Georg's. His final bond with the Society of Jesus brought a new and deeper sense of commitment. He felt carried by his Jesuit brothers' prayers as well as those of his Munich friends, and he increasingly became convinced that the date of Urbi's letter of self-offering, February 15, held a special meaning for him. What it meant was that by then he would be back in Munich, free again.

But first there was a trial to endure. The trial dates had been deferred again and again; who was going to be tried with whom was still an open question. Were they holding out on Delp, hoping to find Rösch and König and thereby hold a Jesuit trial? Then there was the indisputable fact that a single false statement from a man in another prison seemed destined to hang him: the one obstacle preventing him from walking away a free person. He kept racking his brain for ways around his situation.

Finally, in a note from the Mariannes dated January 6, he learned his trial dates had been set for January 9 and 10. He and his Kreisau friends in Tegel would be tried together. They would be driven to the dreaded Gestapo prison on Prinz-Albrechtstrasse the night before the trial, and from there transported to the People's Court.

To M., January 1, 1945

Jesus. The name of our Lord and of my religious order shall be the first word I write in the new year. The name stands for all the things I desire when I pray, believe, and hope; for inner and outer redemption; for relaxation of all the selfish tensions and limitations I place in the way of the free dialogue with God, all the barriers to voluntary partnership and surrender without reserve: and for a speedy release from these horrible fetters. The whole situation is so palpably unjust; things I have neither done nor even known about are keeping me here in prison.

The name Jesus stands also for all that I intended to do in the world, and still hope to do among humanity. To save, to stand by ready to give immediate help, to have goodwill toward all people, and to serve them. I still owe much to so many.

And in conclusion the Society of Jesus, too, is embraced in my invocation of this name—the Society that has admitted me to its membership. May it be personified in me. I have pledged myself to Jesus as his loving comrade and blood brother.

The name stands for passionate faith, submission, selfless effort, and service.

———

To Luise Oestreicher, between January 3 and January 7, 1945

Dear L.,

It's now for certain that the trial is next week, on Tuesday and Wednesday. The miracle lies in reversing the death warrant the men are bringing in their pockets. If that doesn't happen, on Wednesday we'll be standing before God and, if the Lord is gracious, in God's light. . . .

I don't yet feel like writing a farewell letter. Always, when it's a life-or-death situation, I seem to get a courageous sense of certainty. Throughout this whole time, I've never had the feeling of being lost, even though they were saying it to me as they taunted, tormented, and beat me. Somehow the whole shadowy business seemed unreal, having nothing to do with me. But then again there were times when Peter worried about the wind and the waves and began to falter. I'd really never have thought that God would have to work so hard to make me lift my eyes to the mountain.

Everything is now in God's hands. I'll defend myself as much as possible. I hope that physically it will go reasonably well. It's too bad that we're going to be moved from here beforehand. In the other place, we'll be hungry again, and it's a rotten feeling to stand hungry and tired before the power and fury of the offensive. Sometimes I used to say that a piece of bread is a great grace. Now I know from bitter experience.

How it's going to carry on from here, I don't know. Up to now I have only a feeling that I'm going to come through, although I see no real basis for it. Thank everyone for their faithful prayers. I hope you'll all know the date of the trial in time for you to place yourselves beside me. . . .

Now may God protect you. God knows when we'll hear of one another again. I was sometimes a great burden on you. And the worry I've given you since last summer! There could really have been so much more to say. And even more to do. I'd know now how to get things moving. . . .

I wish you God's blessing and protection. He'll have to pay you back for everything I owe you. Greetings to your family and to my friends, and don't forget Secchi. He should think of me a lot during his nights of devotion. But now let's close the window and get on with things. Good-bye.

Georg

To M., January 3, 1945

We are to be here two days more, then we go before the Gestapo. I shall keep the Sacrament with me until then so that I can go on celebrating Mass but I dare not take it with me then as I don't know how thoroughly we shall be searched there and the risk of desecration is too great.

To add to all the rest, I have just learned that the presiding judge is anti-Catholic and a priest-hater; yet another reason for leaving everything confidently in God's hands. It always comes back to this—only he can handle this situation.

During the daytime I read a little Eckhart, the only one of my books I have managed to retain. The whole Eckhart question would be simpler if people remembered that he was a mystic and his mind and soul and spirit were always soaring into higher spheres. He did his best to follow their flight in word and expression—but how can any ordinary mortal succeed in an undertaking that defied even St. Paul? Eckhart failed as, in his own way, every person must fail when it is a matter of analyzing and passing on an intimate personal experience: *individuum est ineffabile* [individuality is inexpressible]. Once we have got back to the point where the ordinary person can have inexpressible secrets, then a favored few will emerge and God will find them sufficiently advanced to draw them into the creative dialogue as he drew Eckhart. With this in mind, reading him becomes more rewarding and more comforting. It gives the reader a glimpse of the divine secret in every human heart.

Tomorrow morning I shall pass on this sheet and there may not be any more before our fate is decided. To be quite honest, if there were any way of escaping that day's ordeal, I should seize it gladly, cowardly as that may sound. That's what it is to be weak. And everything depends on such trifles. The whole business really has no central theme—it just doesn't make sense. If Sperr sticks to his deposition—which is false—there is no hope at all. But what is the use of thinking about it—far better to kneel and pray placing everything in God's hands. *Ad majorem Dei gloriam* [To the greater glory of God].

To Marianne Hapig and Marianne Pünder, January 5, 1945

Good people,

Many thanks for your cleverness and kindness. I do hope we'll soon find the goal we're aiming for. Now comes the real test of faith. On the one hand, the complete freedom to refuse God nothing. On the other, his promise that humble trust has power over him. I haven't looked at my arrest warrant with the nice sentiments on it for weeks now. The whole affair belongs to God. And it isn't just an old tale to say that God doesn't refuse anyone who humbly trusts him. In spite of the seriousness of the situation, I have been consoled in that way again and again. Please keep on having faith and praying with me. Four of us are praying here together, two Catholics and two Protestants, and believing in the wonder of God.

Please take care of the three enclosed letters to Lampertheim—that is, send them to the parish priest, Fr. Heinrich Schäfer, Römerstrasse 43, because I don't know to what extent mail sent directly to family members is inspected. Write to the parish priest and let him know what's happening. I've also enclosed a short letter for him.

Thanks for continuing to provide the Mass wine. I can't have much of it in my cell, always just a small bottle. All the best to you. Thanks a lot—and good-bye. I hope I'll be able to get some writing done on Saturday or Sunday.

Gratefully,

Max

To Franz von Tattenbach, S.J., January 5, 1945

Dear T.,

I've just heard that God has now called Luisette home as well. You know that I'm carrying this sacrifice with you. She was a person whom I was always glad to meet. I have no doubt that she's in God's light. I will gladly bring her into my sacrifice in every sense of that word. Please give my deepest sympathy to your father and sisters. You know that these aren't just words.

This is a hard rule that God has imposed on us to put our authenticity to the test. And sometimes the heart no longer really knows where to find the answers of fidelity and surrender anymore. Left to ourselves, there's no longer any hope. If we ever believed there was, that belief is completely past. God's closed circle and the people inside it keep on helping us, one step at a time. I'll do whatever I can to keep faith with your sister, yourself, and your family.

The hour is striking for me as well; it's still not known whether it will be Monday or Tuesday. We hear both mentioned. It's also not known whether on Monday we'll still be here or at the Gestapo headquarters already. I'd like to have had the lawyer here once more. If we leave on Monday, I might still see him tomorrow, the feast of the Epiphany. Today is the vigil and a First Friday. Nothing has happened yet with regard to Sperr. It seems that that matter is staying open till the very end. *Dios solo basta* is a lofty rule. It makes one broad and free, but sometimes also timid. That's what it is to be human—or rather, that's what it is for me to be human. As Luise recently wrote: consecrated, marked, and sacrificed. . . .

All the best, Tatt. The world is so full of misery and worry that I'm almost ashamed that people are troubling themselves to care about me as well. May God protect you, and thanks.

Georg

———

To M., January 5, 1945

Next week, it seems, my fate will be finally decided. I am full of confidence; God lit an inner light in my soul at Christmas and it has revived my hope. I am already dreaming of my journey home, as excited as any schoolboy. If nothing unexpected happens, I shall be celebrating my last Mass before the trial on the First Friday.

My sister has been very brave; I depend a lot on her prayers and her loyalty. . . . I had not expected her to come until the end of the week.

Things still look very grim but I hope and pray. I have learned a great deal in the past year. God seems much nearer and more real.

Recently I was reading Langbehn.[1] He made it pretty difficult for people to see the truth he was proclaiming among all his general remarks. We used to rave about his work as students. My recent return to it was in many respects a farewell. The outstanding passages really ought to be extracted and collected in an anthology.

——

To M., January 6, 1945

Thank God my fetters were so loosely fastened that tonight I could slip them off again. So I could celebrate Mass exactly as on Christmas Eve with my hands quite free. And this is the last night before the final stage and I am taking the Lord with me after all. The new hiding place the Mariannes have supplied me with is easily disposed of, so God will be with me during the proceedings.

Today the lawyer came to see me again. If all is to go well three things must happen. I have great confidence and my friends will not let me down. This is a moment in which the whole of existence is focused at one point and with it the sum total of reality. I must make my choice and take my stand. The reality of my faith, of God, of the world, of things and their interconnection, of responsibility and the willingness to be answerable for words and actions, as well as the inward urge to fight for existence: all these must be engaged in a single gigantic effort. I have prayed earnestly to God for both kinds of freedom and I shall do so again. After that I will read a little, or perhaps write a little more, till the night guard comes on his round. Then I have to pretend to be asleep.

Sometimes my own reactions puzzle me and I hardly recognize myself. How is it that I can live through these endless hours and days as if the whole wretched misery did not exist? It all seems so unreal. Very often I am not even conscious of it. Then suddenly it all comes back to me. Sometimes I feel like going raving mad and I have to pull myself together. I have to remind myself of the courage of my friends.

To be honest, I am actually more afraid of the actual trial than its possible outcome. Although literally everything is in the balance, I have complete confidence in life; and inwardly too I feel not the slightest temptation to despair.

My neighbor told me I was crazy when I told him that I had to be home by February 15, the day Urbi wrote her letter.

What a miserable scrawl. But the bed is too low and I can't put the chair up to the table because the bed is in the way.

It's too bad that more consultation isn't possible as a result of the bomb damage reports. I'd like to have seen a friendly face before my walk into the arena. . . .

But it's not possible for both of you to come from Munich now, and in any case, Tattenbach has to come to the trial. It will be a good feeling to know that he's praying in the waiting room.

To Maria Delp, January 6, 1945

Dear Mother,

Thank you very much for your greetings. Yesterday Greta was here. She was very kind and brave. I'm glad that you and Marianne are both well. Greta will have told you by now what I think about the various questions (that is, if she managed to get back through Munich).

It seems that the decision will be coming down next week. You'll already know by the time you get these lines. Everything is in God's good hand. And we must give reverence to this hand and be true to it, even if it sometimes grabs us hard. Write often to Father. And be careful not to let Marianne get spoiled. There's a real danger that this might happen.

All the best, dear Mother, and God's blessing to you. Thank you for all your love and kindness and care. I know that you have always wanted the best and done the best for us. Greetings to the good family you're staying with in Munich. Greetings to the teachers in Ecking and everyone in Wolferkam. May God protect you.

Alfred

To Marianne Hapig and Marianne Pünder, January 6, 1945

Good people,

So now it's a matter of praying, praying, and trusting. We mustn't be niggardly and petty toward God, either in giving or in asking and expecting. I've just now heard, for my greater "reassurance," that Freisler is supposed to be a real "priest-hater." That'll be some fun, given this battle zone. If we'd only been able to pull the Sperr problem out beforehand. That way the man wouldn't have been starting off with so many fixed ideas already. But even here there's a meaning, even though it's just a stupid error. It's actually rather laughable that what's tying me up isn't my work at all, but rather a mistake.

Once more, may God reward you both for all your kindness and help. One day you'll certainly realize how much you've put God's greatest commandment into action on our behalf. It's exhausting the way I'm living like Peter here. For a long time the poor guy keeps looking at the water, and then he practically drowns. The time I've spent in this place is a story in itself. There are a lot of wounds, but also a lot of miracles. I've seldom been in more of a cloister, myself with God. May God bless and protect you always.

Max

To M., January 7, 1945

The only opportunity to pass anything on occurs just after exercise—hence just a few more lines.

Yesterday I was more absorbed in contemplating Leonardo da Vinci than the accusations brought against me. I really must study this many-sided and contradictory personality more closely. Many of the puzzling features of modern humanity seem to be encountered in him for the first time—but there are also a few clues for possible solutions. . . .

The man with the irons will soon be here. And tomorrow we are off to the "house of silence." I wish my mother the joy of today's gospel, and that speedily. She has borne enough of sorrow and sacrifice by now. *In nomine Domini.* I have not written any farewell letters; my innermost feelings are beyond utterance.

To Franz von Tattenbach, S.J., January 7, 1945

Dear T.,

Since I don't know if I'll be within reach when you come:

1. Tell the lawyer he should at all costs try to get Gross to come as a witness. His trial will be the day after. He'll do an about-face if he gets a chance.

2. The Sperr mess. It seems that nothing at all has been done. Can't anything be done through the lawyer? I wish

this could have been clarified beforehand because of the psychological prejudice.

3. Thank-you for all your loyalty and kindness. I'm relying a lot on you.

Also: *Dios solo basta.* It's really exhausting, this partnership. And I can well understand how Peter got anxious and afraid once he glanced at the water and away from the Lord.

Say hello to the bosses, colleagues, and friends. God's protection and blessing be with you.

Yours, Georg

———

To Marianne Hapig and Marianne Pünder, shortly before January 9, 1945 (written on a prison order form)

Thanks.

Good-bye!

Pray.

Could I have a small suitcase? Up to now I've been traveling with a paper bag. Is it possible to get hold of some ointment?

CHAPTER II

INFERNO

January 9–January 11, 1945

In his note to the Mariannes shortly before the trial, Delp had asked for a suitcase because he expected that the usual procedure would be followed: that the defendants would be taken to the Gestapo prison on Prinz-Albrechtstrasse the evening before the trial was to begin and reside there until the sentence was handed down. What he mentioned only obliquely was that anyone sentenced to death would be taken immediately to the place of execution, which was a small brick building on the grounds of Plötzensee Prison, near a lake of the same name in north Berlin.

As it turned out, however, Delp did not need the suitcase. A new routine seemed to have come into effect. He and the other three Tegel prisoners to be tried with him—Moltke, Gerstenmaier, and Fugger—were not taken to the Gestapo prison after all, but were driven directly in a police wagon from Tegel to the People's Court on the morning of January 9, the first day of the trial. The other two also to be tried—Franz Sperr and Franz Reisert, a member of Sperr's Bavarian group—were to join them from another prison. Through their secret exchanges, they had agreed on a main line of defense: that they had not taken part in any direct activity against the regime; they had merely discussed constitutional possibilities.

Because the original People's Court had been bombed, the trial took place in a makeshift courtroom inside a public building on Bellevuestrasse. When the four Tegel defendants emerged from the police wagon, Delp caught a glimpse of Tattenbach on the sidewalk. Although his fellow Jesuit, like other friends and relatives of the defendants, would not be allowed into the court itself, Delp felt lifted and carried by this familiar presence nearby.

The small courtroom was located on the second floor. Inside, a long table for the court officials stood at the top of the room. Directly in front of it was a smaller table, before which the defendants were to stand as their turns came. A large Nazi flag hung on the wall facing the assembly, in the center of which a small hole had been made for filming to take place. There were also hidden cameras elsewhere in the room.

The defendants filed in, each flanked by two guards. They sat in four rows facing the front of the room, Delp sitting in the last row. Behind the defendants, assorted Nazi Party members crowded into five rows of chairs. A side door opened, and three officials marched into the room dressed in red robes: the prosecutor, the court clerk, and the president of the People's Court, Judge Roland Freisler. They walked to the long table; Freisler, a fifty-two-year-old man with a thick fringe of black hair surrounding a bald pate, took the center seat.

The disquieting rumors that Delp had heard about Roland Freisler—that he was a priest-hater, that he never changed his mind once the trial began—were true. And there was more. Even within Nazi circles, Freisler had gained a notorious reputation for pitiless and vicious judgments. As a young soldier in World War I, he had been captured by the Russians and had returned to Germany as a member of the Communist Party. After becoming a lawyer, Freisler switched his political allegiance to National Socialism and began his move up through the Nazi ranks. It was said that he had his eye on the post of Minister of Justice. When he was passed over for this position and appointed to the People's Court, he decided to make an indelible impression on Hitler, who was particularly interested in seeing the filmed trials of those associated with the July 20 attack on his life. Freisler's judicial style was to act as both judge and prosecutor and to humiliate the defendants by yelling insults at them. For the trials immediately after July 20 he had outdone himself. Suspenders, belts, and neckties had been removed from the defendants, and they were forced to hold on to their trousers to keep them from falling down. Military stripes had been torn from the jackets of army officers. Freisler shrieked so loudly that at one point a sound engineer warned him that he was wrecking the microphones. When he worked himself into a froth, the blood rose to his face and spread up to his bald head. Not for nothing was the judge nicknamed "Red Roland."

Delp was the first defendant to be called up. He walked to the small table, accompanied by his police guards, who sat down behind him while he stood directly in front of Freisler. The judge began by asking questions in a normal tone of voice that may have momentarily fooled some of the defendants into thinking that he was presiding over a regular court of justice. How had Delp come to know Moltke and Yorck? What did he discuss with them? What did he know of the meetings at Kreisau? What was discussed at these meetings? The Kreisau meetings concerned a future society and yet not one National Socialist was present? Instead there were clergymen and people who later plotted the attempt on the Führer's life? Freisler's voice had begun to rise, his face redden. What did such meetings prove? And the future society they were planning—all this was in the event of a possible defeat?! Defeat?! Such talk amounted to high treason! Freisler now spat out his words, launching into a general tirade: Catholic priests assented to tyrannicide, bishops had fathered illegitimate children, Jesuits provoked an anti-German attitude. In his defense statement, Delp had claimed to have been absent from a meeting that had taken place at his house; this fact was thrown at him as a "typically Jesuitical" action: "By that very absence you show yourself that you knew exactly that high treason was afoot and that you would have liked to keep the tonsured little head, the consecrated holy man, out of it. Meanwhile he may have gone to church to pray that the conspiracy should succeed in a way pleasing to God."[1]

Delp stood calm and self-possessed and spoke in a low, even tone, an effort that he later admitted took every ounce of self-control. The chaplain Harald Poelchau later pieced together an approximate recall of one of the exchanges between Delp and Freisler:

Freisler: "You miserable creep, you clerical nobody—who dares to want the life of our beloved Führer taken . . . a rat—that should be stamped on and crushed. . . . Now tell us, what brought you as a priest to abandon the pulpit and get mixed up in German politics with a subversive like Count Moltke and a troublemaker like the Protestant Gerstenmaier. Come on, answer!"

Delp: "I can preach forever, and with whatever skill I have I can work with people and keep setting them straight. But as long as people have to live in a way that is inhuman and lacking in dignity, that's as long as the average person will succumb to circumstances and will neither pray nor think. A fundamental change in the conditions of life is needed. . . ."

Delp at his trial in the People's Court, January, 1945. Seated behind him is Helmuth von Moltke and, at the far right, Eugen Gerstenmaier. *Courtesy of the Archives of the Upper German Province of the Society of Jesus (Archivum Monacense SJ), Munich.*

Freisler: "Do you mean that the state has to be changed so that you can begin to change conditions that keep people away from the Church?"

Delp: "Yes, that's what I mean. . . ." [2]

Finally, Freisler raised the questions Delp had been dreading: his visit to Stauffenberg and Sperr's incriminating statement about Delp's knowledge of the July 20 plot. But the judge seemed no longer interested. He had made his case against Delp in a volley of personal abuse, and when it came to the main charge against him, Freisler simply waved it away.

Although stung and angered by Freisler's bias against him, Delp may well have been confused by the realization that the indictment he thought would hang him was passed over with hardly a comment. The grilling he had prepared for and fretted over for weeks thus ended abruptly in an anticlimax. The court proceeded to deal with Sperr, Reisert, and Fugger, who comported themselves contritely. At five o'clock the court was dismissed and the accused were driven back to prison. As Delp mulled over the day's proceedings in his cell, the matter became clear to him: his trial had had little to do with the purported reason for his arrest, his supposed involvement with the plot on Hitler's life, about which he had been largely ignorant. He had been on trial and would probably be condemned because of the way of life and the Christian principles to which he had dedicated himself.

That night an official summary was written up of the trial proceedings. About Delp the document stated: "Strong, rustic appearance; trained in dialectical method to an extraordinary degree. Answered neither yes nor no, but constantly sidestepped. To a question of Freisler's, whether he had lied to the police, he answered, 'I did not lie, nor did I not lie.' His action is a classic example of the way Jesuits work. Acted with the knowledge of his provincial superior, who for his part remained throughout in the background. Made possible—according to Freisler's statement—conspiracy meetings at consecrated locations, but during those meetings he himself temporarily disappeared like a madam, so that he could then wash his hands of the matter."[3]

The trial continued the next day, with Moltke and Gerstenmaier as the defendants. As a gesture of courtesy to Moltke's wife, who had asked Freisler personally that her husband be allowed to sit because of his painful sciatica, the judge had a chair provided for him. And then, according to Moltke's account, Freisler proceeded to pour invective. Defeatism! Planning a future German constitution! High treason! Finally came Moltke's most damning activity of all, consorting with Jesuits and with bishops: "A Jesuit Father, and with him of all people you discuss questions of civil disobedience! And you know the Jesuit Provincial too! . . . A Jesuit Provincial, one of the highest officials of Germany's most dangerous enemies. . . . And you're not ashamed of it! No German would touch a Jesuit with a barge-pole! . . . If I know there is a Jesuit Provincial in a town, it is almost a reason for me not to go to that town! . . . And you visit bishops! What is your business with a bishop, with any bishop?"[4]

By the end of the second day, the trial was over. The sentencing was to take place late in the afternoon on the following day. By now Delp was certain of his fate: the prosecution had asked for the death penalty, and he had no doubt that this would be his sentence. He and the others would then be taken immediately to Plötzensee Prison, the place of execution, and within an hour would be dead. When he was brought back to Tegel that evening, he began his farewell letters.

___

To Franz von Tattenbach, S.J., January 10, 1945

Dear Tatt,

Now I really have to write you a farewell letter. I see no other possibility anymore. The Lord wants the sacrifice. All these hard weeks have had as their purpose a training in inner freedom. Up to now he has kept me from breaking down and going into shock. He'll also help me get through the final hours. He often carries me as if I'm a sleeping child.

Thank you very much for everything. We're still sticking together. Give a hearty hello to Knigge. I've just celebrated Mass again. Who else can thus prepare himself these days for this possibility?

The trial was a big farce. From an objective point of view, the main charges—relationship to July 20 and Stauffenberg—weren't raised at all. Sperr had corrected his statement very well. It was a gross insult to the Church and the Society. A Jesuit is and remains a degenerate. It was all a retaliation for Rösch's disappearance and my refusal to renounce my vows. During the proceedings the bedeviling intelligence and energy of a Jesuit were especially emphasized. The trial bristled with abusive comments toward the Church and its organizations. Scandals, bishops who were supposed to have had children, etc.; the Latin language, Jesuits' corrupt dealings, etc.—this kind of thing came up in every other sentence. Objectively, I was able to say what I wanted; but no one believes a Jesuit because he is on principle an enemy of the Reich and above all an enemy of the Nazi Party. For this reason the judgment against the people who knew Goerdeler and had spoken with him was more lenient than it was for me.

Moltke was also given dreadful abuse because of his relationship with the Church and the Jesuits. A Moltke next to a Jesuit is a shameful and debased human being. What I've already experienced at the hands of the Gestapo I noticed here again: this intense onslaught of hatred against the Church and the Society. So now at least my work has achieved an authentic goal.

Love and best wishes to you. Please take care of my family a bit. May God protect you. Good-bye.

Gratefully,

Alfred Delp

To Luise Oestreicher, January 11, 1945

Dear Luise,

This now has to be a farewell letter. God seems to want me to make the full sacrifice and to take the other road. They've asked for the death sentence, and the atmosphere is so full of hate and hostility that I can't see any other way. The whole trial was driven by hate and hostility. When it came to the points of actual incrimination, the charge fell. But from the first word I knew that the verdict was already decided. Right now my interior position is rather strange. Although I know that if things follow their normal course I'm going to die tonight, I'm not feeling bad at all. Perhaps God is being gracious and sparing me the fear of death up to the end. Or am I supposed to keep on believing that a miracle is going to happen? *Adoro* and *Suscipe* were the last words of the Epiphany reflection I wrote for you. Let's leave ourselves there. Don't be sad. . . . Pray for me and I'm going to help you as well, you'll see. Now I have to let go completely. Thanks for all your love and kindness and loyalty. And don't hold my moods and immaturity and harshness and nastiness against me.

Greetings to my friends. Whatever happens, it's being offered as seed planted in the earth, and as blessing and sacrifice. God bless you. Now you're going to have two brothers as guardian angels.

In the enclosed envelope are bits of newspaper, etc. During my loneliest hours I tore these off from what I had for toilet paper so that I could write some words of reflection. I wanted to attach them to a sheet and write something further, and then give them to you as a gift.

May God protect you. Keep up your courage. Thank you and good-bye.

Alfred

To Maria Delp, January 11, 1945

Dear Mother,

I now have to write you the hardest letter that a child has ever had to write to his mother. It's all become so hopeless that I have to presume I'll be sentenced to death and then executed. Keep your courage up, dear Mother. It's God who decides our fate. We want to give ourselves to him without being spiteful. It's hard on you, dear Mother, but it has to be endured.

Thank you so much for all your love and kindness. You've had such loving concern for us and have done and suffered so much for us. Thank you from the bottom of my heart for every single thing that you've given me and that you've been for me.

Best greetings to Father. I don't think I'll write directly to him. He'll have to be gradually prepared. Just tell him thank-you from me for everything, from the bottom of my heart.

Keep up your courage, dear Mother. Pray for me. When I'm with God, I'll pray and plead on your behalf and make up for all the love I've withheld.

We'll see each other again. After a little while we'll be together again. And then it will be forever and filled with God's joy.

God protect you, *Mutterl*. Take care that Marianne grows up in the right way. I'll also keep an eye on her. All the best to you.

Your grateful

Alfred

To Marianne Hapig and Marianne Pünder, January 11, 1945

Good people,

Well, so now I'm going down the other road. Whatever God wills. Let it all be done and given over into his freedom and goodness.

May God reward you for all your kindness and love. That was no court of law, but rather an orgy of hate. . . .

The incriminating points in the initial charge didn't stand.

The way the trial was carried out has provided my life with its true life-and-death purpose. The grounds for the charge that came up at the trial boiled down to the following four incriminations (everything else is rubbish; it's important that there was no connection to July 20, etc.):

1. Thinking about a future for Germany after a possible defeat ("We will all die together, the last German, the Nazi party, the Third Reich, and the German people"— Freisler).

2. The incompatibility between Nazism and Christianity. Thus my thinking was false and dangerous, because it was based on this conviction (the "re-Christianizing idea" that they've accused Moltke of is an "attack against Germany").

3. The Society of Jesus is a threat and any Jesuit is a degenerate. We're fundamentally an enemy of Germany.

4. Catholic teaching on *iustitia socialis* [social justice] as the basis for a future socialism.

The trial has been recorded. Perhaps it will have some use at the appropriate time. If I have to die, at least I know why. Who else among the many others dying these days knows that much? We're dying as witnesses to these four truths, and if I'm allowed to live, I know as well what my sole purpose will be in the future. Greetings to everyone I know.

Thanks so much for everything. Letters can still get by through Buchholz. Please look after that for me. In particular, send the list of belongings to Munich so that my things don't get taken away. I haven't felt any fear up to now. God is good. Please pray. I'll answer from there.

Good-bye.

Georg

To his fellow Jesuits, January 11, 1945

Dear Brothers,

Here I am at the parting of the ways and I must take the other road after all. The death sentence has been passed and the atmosphere is so charged with enmity and hatred that no appeal has any hope of succeeding.

I thank the Society and my brothers for all their goodness and loyalty and help, especially during these last weeks. I ask pardon for much that was untrue and unjust; and I beg that a little help and care may be given to my aged, sick parents.

The actual reason for my condemnation was that I happened to be, and chose to remain, a Jesuit. There was nothing to show that I had any connection with the attempt on Hitler's life, so I was acquitted on that count. . . . The rest of the accusations were far less serious and more factual. There was one underlying theme—a Jesuit is a priori an enemy and betrayer of the Reich. Moltke was treated abominably as well because he was associated with us, especially with Rösch. So the whole proceedings turned into a sort of comedy developing a theme. It was not justice—it was simply the carrying out of the determination to destroy.

May God protect you all. I ask for your prayers. And I will do my best to catch up, on the other side, with all that I have left undone here on earth.

Toward noon I will celebrate Mass once more and then in God's name take the road under his providence and guidance.

In God's blessing and protection,

Your grateful Alfred Delp, S.J.

CHAPTER 12

AFTER THE TRIAL

January 11–January 21, 1945

In the late afternoon of Thursday, January 11, with his farewell letters completed, Delp was brought back to the People's Court with the other five defendants for the verdict and sentencing. They were pushed into an anteroom, and then led, handcuffed, into the courtroom. The sentences were read with little ceremony: death by hanging for Delp, Moltke, and Sperr; prison sentences for Fugger, Reisert, and Gerstenmaier (Gerstenmaier had succeeded in presenting himself as a naive and bumbling preacher).

Delp showed no emotion when his sentence was read out, but, in the police van immediately afterward, his composure broke and a flash of the out-of-control wildness of former years burst out. He fell into a frenzy of laughter, sputtering one-liners between manic gasps. (To Gerstenmaier, whom Freisler had labeled a "blockhead,": "Better a blockhead than no head at all.")[1] The others sat subdued and still.

To everyone's surprise, the three condemned to death were not taken to Plötzensee Prison to be executed but were driven back to Tegel. They were taken to their cells, locked up, and left alone as if nothing had happened. It now seemed, once again, as if there still might be some hope.

The hours became days, and a sort of normalcy returned: the shackled wrists, the oppressive night hours, the blazing light and indecipherable prison sounds. And, during the interminable hours of the day, opportunity for deeper reflection. With paper and ink that the Mariannes continued to provide, Delp wrote a final testament, "After the Verdict," to be distributed clandestinely among his friends.

His emotions seesawed from moment to moment: *They're going to hang me; I don't think they'll hang me. Maybe I'll live after all!* Was God testing him to the limit with this brief reprieve? With God's help, he would prove equal to the test. And he would return to Munich from this nightmare forever changed. The Third Reich was in a state of near collapse, and every day brought Russian troops closer and closer to Berlin's city limits. One of these days, the prison doors would be thrown open and his hands untied. But then the emotional thud: he was headed for execution, planted as a seed in the ground, and desperate for the prayers of his friends to keep him from the despair that seemed ready to swallow him. Why couldn't they have put the noose around his neck right away and be done with it? What was God's mysterious purpose in this terrible zigzag of events?

A new surge of life and creativity began to flow, and what emerged was a meditation on the Our Father. Once again, the meditation begins with his own situation: the metaphor he uses this time is a mountain cliff, where he breathes rarified air, bereft even of the comforting whispers during the circle-walks, which no longer occur. His companions also sit condemned to death and isolated in adjoining cells on their own mountain cliffs. The word *Our* of the Our Father brings the realization that there is a bridge between him and his friends that no cruel system can tear down, a bridge on which one encounters another, through God, within an atmosphere of adoration. Only by acknowledging God for who

God is, he says, can one become one's true self and enter true dialogue. *Give us this day our daily bread. . . .* He returns to his thoughts of former years on Christian society and his emphasis on the necessity for minimum social standards before adoration can take place. Then he returns to himself on his mountain cliff: the human person alone, facing God. "Life is a contest," he writes, reflecting on the final passage of the prayer. "Deliver us from evil. Wherever self is stressed, as in strength that glories in its own might, power that idolizes itself, life that aims at 'fulfilling itself' in its own way and by its own resources, in all these, not the truth, but the negation of truth may be suspected." [2] One must surrender, finally, and pray for deliverance.

Some days later, he wrote to Luise Oestreicher that he was sending on some reflections on the Pentecost sequence, "Come, Holy Spirit." The letter says that he has written it especially for her and Tattenbach. And for himself, he adds. He begins this meditation with the word *Come*: the cry of hunger and thirst. The creative dialogue between God and humanity takes place through the Holy Spirit. Without God we are nothing, we are wasted lives, he writes. It is easy to imagine Delp looking at the crumbs of his own life, now nearing its bitter end. "Help comes from the hills," he says again and again, as on his lonely mountain cliff, at every moment at risk of falling into despair, he continues to cling. [3] "God alone suffices": he says this as well, again and again, as if willing the words to penetrate his own psyche. [4] God brings us through this calamity, and we will see that in the very calamity itself light and strength are found. "Blessed are those," he finishes, returning to his original thought, "who hunger and thirst": the desire for God is the pathway to freedom. [5]

In the meantime, the days continued on their dull pace. He wondered how his friends were faring during the bomb attacks. He was concerned about the ill health of the head guard who had been kind to him: could the Mariannes come up with some medicine to help the man? And communicating through order-form notes, the Mariannes brought up the question of an appeal. He considered this a futile exercise, but telling them that he lacked all perspective in the matter himself, he took their advice and wrote a letter of appeal to the chief justice.

Eventually, after debating the matter with himself, he also decided to write a special plea for clemency to Himmler, who had been in school with one of the Munich Jesuits. In the letter, he cited his lack of involvement with July 20, no proven intentions of violence toward the Third Reich, his family's contribution to Germany's side in the war: his brothers, Ewald and Fritz, soldiers and now prisoners of war; his brothers-in-law, one killed in action, another missing in action, a third on the Western front. More and more personal contacts occurred to him—anyone at all he knew of who might have some influence with the regime—and he scribbled these names down in letters to the two Mariannes, Luise Oestreicher, and Tattenbach. He was certain that there would be no reprieve, but a bureaucratic delay from some quarter might buy him time.

He was to learn during the two weeks after the trial that on January 11, the same day that he received the death sentence, Augustin Rösch had been caught and arrested. (An informer had tipped off the Gestapo that Rösch was hiding on a farm owned by a man named Wolfgang Meier, east of Munich. He had been taken to the Dachau concentration camp along with four members of the Meier family and a local parish priest. From Dachau, he had been brought to a Gestapo prison in Berlin and, in transit, persuaded a guard to get the word of his arrest to his friends in Tegel.) Rösch was now undergoing the same intensive interrogations that Delp

The Meier family. Wolfgang Meier Sr. (seated front, right) died in the concentration camp at Dachau. *Courtesy of the Archives of the Upper German Province of the Society of Jesus (Archivum Monacense SJ), Munich.*

had suffered. Was this why he was being kept alive, Delp wondered, to be brought face to face with his fellow Jesuit in a new round of questioning? If so, would it be possible to let Rösch know the strategy the other Kreisau members had agreed on during their weeks of prison circle-walks? He hoped Rösch could withstand the beatings and not break down.

Once more, there were visits from his sister Greta and from Tattenbach. When he walked into the small visiting room where Greta sat waiting, he blurted out, before the guard could stop him from speaking about the trial, "They're going to hang me."[6] The visit was strained; words hung in the air. Then, with hardly a word of farewell, Delp jumped up from his chair, turned, and left. (For years afterward, Greta Kern recounted her final memory of her brother: the sight of the back of his head disappearing into the blackness of the prison interior, and her own longing for a final look back, a wave of good-bye that never came.)

The sight of Tattenbach's thin face, exhausted from lack of food and sleep and anxious with frantic concern, touched Delp to the core. Was his one life worth the effort his faithful friend was expending? And yet Tattenbach, now even more than the Mariannes, seemed to be the one link to whatever means there might be left to free him.

———

To M., after January 11, 1945

After the Verdict

It has become an odd sort of life I am leading. It is so easy to get used to existence again that one has to keep reminding oneself that death is round the corner. Condemned to death. The thought refuses to penetrate; it almost needs force to drive it home. The thing that makes this kind of death so singular is that one feels so vibrantly alive with the will to live unbroken and every nerve tingling with life. A malevolent external force is the only thing that can end it. The usual intimations of approaching death are therefore lacking. One of these days the door will open, the guard will say, "Pack up. The car will be here in half an hour." We have often heard this and know exactly what it is like.

Actually, I had thought to be taken to Plötzensee straight away last Thursday evening. But a new timetable is in force and we, apparently, are the first people to come under it. Or could it be that appeals have been made? I hardly think so. Here everything is subjective—not even bureaucratic procedure but undisguised subjectivity. The man Freisler is able, nervous, vain, and arrogant.

He is playing a part and his opponent must be made to look inferior. In this sort of dialogue the advantage of having the upper hand is obvious.

While it was all going on, I felt as if I were a mere spectator. It was rather like a bad Pullach debate, only that the defense kept changing and the accuser decided who was in the right. His fellow judges, the "people," were a bunch of ordinary, dutiful individuals who had put on their Sunday suits very ceremoniously for the occasion and took themselves very seriously indeed, sitting there in judgment with Herr President in his red robe. They were good biddable SS men, obediently fulfilling the role of the "people"— which is to say "yes."

Everything was as per schedule—nothing missing; the Grand Entrance with an awe-inspiring muster of police—each of us had two men with him. Behind us, the public, mostly Gestapo and so on; their faces are good-natured, average faces, very accustomed to this sort of thing, the average type representing "the" Germany. The other Germany is not represented, or is in the process of being condemned to death. All the performance needed was an overture and a finale at the end—or at least a fanfare.

The proceedings themselves were handled slickly and ruthlessly— so ruthlessly that no word in the defendants' favor was even permitted. The only questions asked were those that suited the accusers' purpose and the findings, naturally, were in accordance.

Our case was aimed at the destruction of Moltke and myself and all the rest was mere window-dressing. I knew from the moment we began that my fate was already sealed. The questions were all prepared and followed a definite plan and woe betide any answer that did not fit into the prearranged pattern. Scholasticism and Jesuitism were paraded as the real villains. It is a common belief that a Jesuit commits a crime every time he draws breath.

He can say and do and prove whatever he likes—no one ever believes him. . . .

The slanders on the Church, incidents singled out from Church history, the smirching of the Society of Jesus, and so on were very grim. I had to keep a tight grip on myself to stop myself from exploding. But if I had let go it would have ruined all our chances. It was a great opportunity for the actor to declare his opponent a clever, dangerous, beaten man and then show off as being, himself, immensely superior. From the moment he started it was all over. I strongly advise my brothers in the Society to keep away from these trials where one is not a human being but an object. And all under an inflated rigmarole of legal terms and phrases. Just before this I had been reading Plato, who said that the greatest injustice is that performed in the name of justice.

Our own crime was that of heresy against the Third Reich. . . . Someone ought to remind Freisler what would have happened if Moltke's defense plan had been used. And how many of the men he has condemned are being missed now. Anyone who dares cast any doubts on the Nazi system is of course a heretic—and former judgments on heretics are child's play compared with the refined and deadly retribution practiced by these people.

Moltke's plight might not have been so bad if he had not been "tied up with the Church," which laid him open to the charge of "re-Christianizing intentions." He had consorted with bishops and Jesuits. What fools we were when we tried to make preparation for this trial—it had nothing whatever to do with facts or truth. This was not a court of justice but a function. An unmistakable echo and nothing else. I just can't understand how anyone can go on doing this sort of thing day after day.

The final session was on Thursday and all around everything else went on as usual—rather like a prize-giving in a small school that hadn't even the proper room for it. I thought Moltke and I would be taken to Plötzensee immediately afterward, but we are still here in Tegel.

The sentence seemed just as unreal as the proceedings of the two previous days. I kept the Host with me and before the final session I said Mass, and communion was my last meal. I wanted to be prepared. But here I am, still waiting.

Up to now the Lord has helped me wonderfully. I am not yet scared and not yet beaten. The hour of human weakness will no doubt come and sometimes I am depressed when I think of all the things I hoped to do. But I am now a man internally free and far more genuine and realized than I was before. Only now have I sufficient insight to see the thing as a whole.

To be quite honest, I do not yet believe in my execution. I don't know why. Perhaps God our Father has some great grace in store for me and will enable me to pass through this wilderness without having to perish in it. During the proceedings, even when it was clear there would be no miracle, I felt lifted above it all and quite untouched by all that was going on. Was that a miracle? If not, what was it? I am really in some embarrassment before God and must think it out.

All these long months of misfortune fit into some special pattern. From the first I was so sure everything would turn out well. God always strengthened me in that conviction. These last few days I have doubted and wondered whether my will to live has been sublimated into religious delusions or something like that. Yet all these unmistakable moments of exaltation in the midst of misery; my confidence and unshakable faith even when I was being beaten up, the certain "in spite of it all" that kept my spirits up and made me so sure that they would not succeed in destroying me; those consolations in prayer and in the Blessed Sacrament, the moments of grace; the signs I prayed for that were vouchsafed again and again—must I put them all away from me now?—Does God ask the sacrifice which I will not deny him, or is he testing my faith and my trust to the last limit of endurance? As I was being taken to Berlin for the preliminary hearing, I suddenly remembered the unexploded bomb in St. Ignatius's House and quite distinctly I heard the words, "It will not explode. . . ."

And the second special thing about this week is that everything I did to better my situation went wrong and in fact made it worse. It was the same during the recent hearing. The change of lawyers, which at first seemed so promising, was a bad mistake. As the new man became aware of the anti-Jesuit complex he told me, while the proceedings were still in progress, that as a matter of fact he was against Jesuits too. Sending Freisler the small book *Humanity and History* was a mistake also—it only gave him the impression I was clever and therefore more dangerous. Statistics prepared for our defense were used against us. The whole proceedings led to one disaster after another. And on top of all this the quite unforeseen misfortune that we remain here, still alive, when we had prepared ourselves to die last Thursday. And so on.

What is God's purpose in all this? Is it a further lesson with regard to complete freedom and absolute surrender? Does he want us to drain the chalice to the dregs and are these hours of waiting preparation for an extraordinary Advent? Or is he testing our faith?

What should I do to remain loyal—go on hoping despite the hopelessness of it all? Or should I relax? Ought I to resign myself to the inevitable and is it cowardice not to do this and to go on hoping? Should I simply stand still, free and ready to take whatever God sends? I can't yet see the way clear before me; I must go on praying for light and guidance. And then there is the accepted sacrifice of the past seven months. It is terrible the way

I keep on going over these things in my heart. But at least I will look at them honestly under the impulse of the Holy Spirit.

When I compare my icy calm during the court proceedings with the fear I felt, for instance, during the bombing of Munich, I realize how much I have changed. But the question keeps coming back—was this change the purpose of it all—or is this inner exaltation and help the miracle I asked for?

I don't know. Logically there is no hope at all. The atmosphere here, so far as I am concerned, is so hostile that an appeal has not the slightest chance of succeeding. So is it madness to hope—or conceit, or cowardice, or grace? Often I just sit before God looking at him questioningly.

But one thing is gradually becoming clear—I must surrender myself completely. This is seedtime, not harvest. God sows the seed and some time or other he will do the reaping. The one thing I must do is to make sure the seed falls on fertile ground. And I must arm myself against the pain and depression that sometimes almost defeat me. If this is the way God has chosen—and everything indicates that it is—then I must willingly and without rancor make it my way. May others at some future time find it possible to have a better and happier life because we died in this hour of trial.

I ask my friends not to mourn, but to pray for me and help me as long as I have need of help. And to be quite clear in their own minds that I was sacrificed, not conquered. It never occurred to me that my life would end like this. I had spread my sails to the wind and set my course for a great voyage, flags flying, ready to brave every storm that blew. But it could be they were false flags or my course wrongly set or the ship a pirate and its cargo contraband. I don't know. And I will not sink to cheap jibes at the world in order to raise my spirits. To be quite honest I don't want to die, particularly now that I feel I could do more important work and deliver a new message about values I have only just discovered and understood. But it has turned out otherwise. God keep me in his providence and give me strength to meet what is before me.

It only remains for me to thank a great many people for their help and loyalty and belief in me, and for the love they have shown me. First and foremost my brothers in the Society who gave me a genuine and beautiful vision of life. And the many sincere people I was privileged to meet. I remember very clearly the times when we were able to meet freely and discuss the tasks in front of us. Do not give up, ever. Never cease to cherish the people in your hearts—the poor forsaken and betrayed people who are so helpless. For in spite of all their outward display and loud self-assurance, deep down they are lonely and frightened. If through one life there is a little more love and kindness, a little more light and truth in the world, then that life will not have been in vain.

Nor must I forget those to whom I owe so much. May those I have hurt forgive me—I am sorry for having injured them. May those to whom I have been untrue forgive me—I am sorry for having failed them. May those to whom I have been proud and overbearing forgive me—I repent my arrogance. And may those to whom I have been unloving forgive me—I repent my hardness. Oh yes—long hours spent in this cell with fettered wrists and my body and spirit tormented must have broken down a great deal that was hard in me. Much that was unworthy and worthless has been committed to the flames.

So farewell. My offense is that I believed in Germany and her eventual emergence from this dark hour of error and distress, that I refused to accept that accumulation of arrogance, pride, and force that is the Nazi way of life, and that I did this as a Christian and a Jesuit. These are the values for which I am here now on the brink, waiting for the thrust that will send me over. Germany will be reborn, once this time has passed, in a new form based on reality with Christ and his Church recognized again as being the answer to the secret yearning of this earth and its people, with the Society of Jesus the home of proven men—men who today are hated because they are misunderstood in their voluntary dedication or feared as a reproach in the prevailing state of pathetic, immeasurable human bondage. These are the thoughts with which I go to my death.

And so to conclude, I will do what I so often did with my fettered hands and what I will gladly do again and again as long as I have a breath left—I will give my blessing. I will bless this land and the people; I will bless the Church and pray that her fountains may flow again fresher and more freely; I will bless all those who have believed in me and trusted me, all those I have wronged and all those who have been good to me—often too good.

God be with you and protect you. Help my poor old parents through these days of trial and keep them in your thoughts. God help you all.

I will honestly and patiently await God's will. I will trust him till they come to fetch me. I will do my best to ensure that this blessing, too, shall not find me broken and in despair.

To Luise Oestreicher, after January 11, 1945

Dear L.,

Many thanks for your Christmas letter. . . . I'm sitting on my cliff, focused totally on God and his freedom. And I'm relying on him. On the 11th I wrote my good-byes. According to the way it's been done up to now, we should have been dead on the evening of the 11th. We're now just sitting here and waiting. If we had been tried before Christmas, it would have been done the old way. Because of the way this trial was conducted, my life has been given a theme for which I might live or die. There are four points on which I've been charged, and whether I'm to die for them, or whether they're simply the basis of a mission for which I'm being prepared—it doesn't really matter. I'm condemned because I believe in Germany in spite of the roaring night out there, because I believe in the Church as a guiding force for this people, because I belong to the Society of Jesus, and because I want to serve what I've seen, that is, social justice, which is rising from the people's misery and from the Church's message. Who of the many being killed these days is falling for so much? And knows it? I was charged on these four counts, and I'm being condemned because of them. If it's meant as a preparation for mission, then the theme is evident. Since the 11th the world has changed. . . . It is no longer a world of idylls, and this is so regardless of whether I end up in Plötzensee or return to Munich. I'm relying on you. Thanks and greetings and love and blessing.

Georg

(Don't let my mother tell any "pious legends" about me. I was a brat.)

You will have received the Our Father. I've begun writing a few thoughts on the Pentecost prayer for you. And I'd like to finish the litany. I hope to find a few words for you and my friends. Incidentally, a miracle can still happen. When I consider the special guidance so far, it's obvious: God holds this affair entirely in his hand. Perhaps he wants to be sure I'm persevering in my reliance on him. May God protect you. The man is coming with the handcuffs.

G.

Continuing with the handcuffs. I want to write you just another short greeting. Together with this note I'm sending some pages with the litany and several pages of the Pentecost prayer. I hope you find joy in them. Check the spelling; most of them were written in handcuffs. May God protect you. Good-bye.

Georg

The next day: Show Tattenbach the letter from Helmuth that I sent you for safekeeping. I've told him that he can ask you for it. I've written the Pentecost sequence especially for you and Tattenbach, the two people who have taken so much trouble and have carried such a heavy burden on my behalf. I often send you my blessing with handcuffed hands—a blessing which no one can shackle. . . .

Greetings to my friends. How are Annemarie and Emmi? Best wishes. Best wishes also to our summer friends from the Prinzregentstrasse. And Chrysolia. I thank her for her greetings, which have just arrived. And her prayer. And keep on praying, as long as I can still breathe. And even more so afterward. Good-bye.

———

To Marianne Hapig and Marianne Pünder, after January 11, 1945

Good people,

Please don't worry. I'm neither reproaching God nor accusing him. The trial was given a perfect theme because of the nature of the proceedings and its clear intent against the Church and the Society of Jesus. It was difficult to hold onto myself and not lose control over those wild insults. It's too bad that the proceeding is a "secret Reich matter." Within this atmosphere, which is entirely manufactured by the Gestapo, attempts and petitions here in Berlin are almost hopeless. The only possibility would be to approach Himmler through the Munich connections and explain Moltke's deliberations to him. My case is favorable in that I was completely acquitted of any connection to July 20, which was the reason for my arrest and the charges against me. Himmler is not doing much for cases related to July 20. We must pass this matter on very quickly to Tattenbach. He will know what the possibilities are: "Hitler's mother" (contact: Colonel Wurms, Dr. Schmitt, P. Körbling)—Director Weidemann's wife (contact: Dr. Kessler)—also speak with the lawyer Paepcke in the United Workshops. He knows many highly placed Party members through his father's business. The grunt of an SA man is worth more than a hundred pieces of evidence. Even the Party connections in Bogenhausen would be valuable: Grassl, the local branch through Colonel Müller, perhaps also Princess Wittgenstein or her son-in-law: contact: Prell. I'm mentioning all of them for my mother's sake. Thank you very much.

Max

To Pastor Max Blumschein (pastor of Precious Blood parish in Bogenhausen), after January 11, 1945

Dear fatherly friend, may I call you that?

Now that conditions as well as the guidance and providence of God have led me to the threshold, many matters reveal themselves more simply and clearly in the Lord as they are and were. In any case, I would not like to depart without a word of thanks to you for so much kindness, patience, and consideration. In Bogenhausen I had a good apprenticeship and a tough time as a journeyman. The master's exam, which I wasn't able to take there, I have to complete here. Gladly and often I think of the wonderful times and the hard times we spent together. Gladly and often are prayers and blessings directed there with my bound hands. May God express thanks for me and make up for my foolishness, for which my debt remains. God's blessing and grace always to you, your people, and your parishioners. Thank you very much, and good-bye.

Georg

To Maria Delp, January 14, 1945

Dear Mother,

A heartfelt Sunday greeting. I'm still alive, though in the normal course of events, Thursday should have been my last day. How many days or hours or weeks God is still giving me, I don't know. We don't want to be angry with him, Mother. You will have received last Thursday's letter from me.

Stay brave and steadfast, Mother. Up to now I'm doing very well. I have great peace and no anxiety. God can always work miracles. This is the one thing: pray and trust more and more. We are not allowed to deny him anything. This is the other: be ready for anything that he wills and sends. To fall as the good seed into the earth. And to go home as a blessing for you all. Many devoted thanks to you for your love and goodness. Forgive me for the worry I have caused you.

Good-bye.

Alfred

———

To Franz von Tattenbach, S.J., January 14, 1945

Dear Tatt,

Things always turn out differently from what one thinks and expects. In the first place, the trial was faithful to its original logic and came to its expected conclusion. Secondly, we weren't executed on the same day we were convicted, as has been customary up to now regardless of the plea for clemency, but are still here. My neighbor, sentenced the following day but without a plea for clemency, is also still here. We seem to be the first who came to the trial, not to the Gestapo. If we had been tried before Christmas, all this would have happened differently.

How are matters continuing now? The normal course will be toward Plötzensee. From here, that's a ten-minute drive. One is picked up a quarter of an hour before execution. Mentally, I'm not quite clear. See the pages, "After the Verdict." I know and have somehow always known that my present situation is an important part of my life. I have a kind of inner sense of such things. Whether the drive to Plötzensee is part of it, I don't know yet. On Thursday I was completely resigned to go to Plötzensee, because it was the normal thing to happen, and one didn't expect anything different. Given the atmosphere in the court, it was impossible for it not to happen. Particularly because that guy isn't clever, but is crafty and vain and theatrical. Even so, that morning

I said to the guard, who was weeping, "Be quiet, we're not going to die today."

But to remain in the freedom of God: for hours, days, or weeks, according to his will. There are two here from July 20 who have already been waiting fourteen weeks since their conviction. Is anyone attending to the pleas? It's important that we separate ourselves from July 20. Our own problem was labeled "run-of-the-mill high treason." I believe that help is possible only through a Party connection. But only if the atmosphere gets somewhat cleansed at the top. Schmeo (Dr. Schmitt) or your aunt or the wife of the colonel from Nymphenberg or Zeller of Hammerau (can be reached through Schmeo and Alfons) could get Christian to act. What are the chances of a plea by the Moltke family? They couldn't very well pardon my "leader" and hang his "youngest and most faithful colleague." In fact, though, they can do anything. Logic leads nowhere except to Plötzensee. Since last night I've been hoping and trusting more positively again. I haven't given up, but for a while I felt bitter and flat. Tatt, as hopeless as the situation is and as much as God knows that I'm refusing him nothing but am continuing to struggle so that I'll fall into the ground as fruitful and nourishing seed: yet I don't believe I'm headed for the gallows. Perhaps it's only a "remedial lesson" that God is using to help me through the situation. I had to stifle a loud laugh at the verdict because it was such a farce. Somehow it didn't touch me, although after the verdict I thought I'd be on my way. The Gestapo man, thinking that I was weak and broken, asked me slyly about Rösch and König. That confirmed my belief that they would, as they had done with the others before us, carry out the verdict immediately. I sent greetings to Rösch through the Gestapo man. He was

astonished at my "weakness." I know well that the hour of
the creature will still come. It went well for Reisert, as I always
said. . . .

Actually, we must do what we can for Moltke. He has been
badly incriminated because of his contact with us, and therefore
has been treated in an ugly manner. Can't we once again raise the
issue of Moltke's plans to a higher forum? Particularly since my
life is now hanging on these matters as well? I'm attaching a
sketch of these plans and a description of how they were twisted
during the prosecution.

Now, heartfelt thanks and God's blessing. Fix up what I failed
to accomplish. *Adoro et Suscipe* I wrote in the Epiphany
meditation. It continues to be true. This is what remains, even
beyond Plötzensee. Greetings to your people.

Your grateful Georg

I don't think those people will pardon me. There is simply too
much hatred toward the Jesuits. But perhaps in spite of this a
miracle will happen. Perhaps the meaning of all the interruptions is
only this: to gain time. Perhaps God will test my trust up to the very
last. That's also all right with me. Life in any case has been given a
leitmotif. And solace in the face of anxiety is a miracle in itself.

To Greta Kern, January 16, 1945

Dear Greta,

Thank you for coming. Don't be angry at me for making it so
short. I'm happy to see that you're so brave. And that you still

have hope. I still have hope too. Either God wants my life or he wants to teach me a lesson. In neither case must we say "No." And whoever isn't able to accept death hasn't lived right. Death isn't an assault, a foreign power, but rather the last part of this life. The two are connected.

Let's keep on praying and hoping, no matter what God decrees. . . . God protect you. Good-bye.

Alfred

———

To Luise Oestreicher, January 18, 1945

Dear Luise,

Greetings once again. And I wanted to tell you to get together with Greta. You will like each other and can help one another.

I'm doing well. God has never before left me so much in the dark. But I'm going to remain steadfast. Either he wants the sacrifice or he wants to test my trust right up to the breaking point. I intend to keep on trying. Either he is sowing me as a seed or he is directing me toward some great work. The normal measure of things doesn't count anymore, not after January 11. But you are helping me pray and remain steadfast, aren't you? Despite everything, I have a positive feeling that doesn't originate from myself. When I consider how he carried me during the three days, from the 9th to the 11th—and how a few weeks ago, when it occurred to me for the first time that this might be my destiny, and then to have to wait—what fear gripped me in the face of this possibility—and how he is now holding me and leading me. Thank you for everything. . . . I have brought a lot of worry into your life; may it be a blessed and consecrated worry. Greetings to everyone. Blessings and heartfelt greetings to you.

Georg

To Franz von Tattenbach, S.J., January 18, 1945

Dear Tatt,

I'm still alive. A week ago I got ready for a good departure and was expecting it at any time. It's all so strange. We are among the first not to have been executed immediately after the verdict. It was a great joy to see you there. The atmosphere was evil. The stage was set so clearly against the Church and against Christianity that from now on because of these two days our life has been given a reason to live or die. And the whole thing was the final break with all the measures and regulations that have existed up to now and that during the last few weeks have already been subject to all kinds of exceptions. You are right, friend— even if I come back, the world is different because of January 11. Things will never be the same again. An interior strength allows me more and more hope and confidence. As I sit here on call, though, I certainly don't want to minimize the situation and have convulsions doing it. The time for convulsions is definitely past (in Plötzensee, they're only physiological, and therefore don't count). I'm living in great peace and freedom, I'm praying, and yesterday and today I wrote a few thoughts on the Our Father, almost entirely in shackles and thus it's even more illegible than usual. As far as the petitions are concerned, do what you want. Perhaps the final salutary humiliation is to have to accept life as grace. Perhaps the whole purpose is to wait and in the meantime *tempus acceptabile* [the acceptable time] happens. *Deus scit* [God knows]. My existence depends entirely on him. Actually, the whole trial seemed to be much more a mission than an end for Moltke and me. And perhaps all that has happened as a result of July 20 has its own meaning. Thanks for your good letter. Has God made use of the highest authorities of the Third Reich in order for me to make something of my inner self? Greetings to the brothers and to your family. God protect you.

Bullus

To Marianne Hapig and Marianne Pünder, January 21, 1945

. . . I'm here, in the most extreme situation possible for a human being. That is, everything human is pushed to the extreme. You're helping me, aren't you, so that breath doesn't leave me? I've been offered a big grace of freedom and a vast space. May I never let it pass me by or wither. Greetings to my friends. I thank them for their greetings, which have arrived, and for their prayer. I ask that it continue, for as long as I'm breathing. And even more so afterward.

Georg

To the Kreuser family, January 21, 1945

Dear Friends,

Getting into heaven is an exhausting business. I should have been there a week ago, and yet I'm still here. May God repay you for all your help and goodness. Just now Tattenbach was here. At that point, everything became clear and concrete again. How gladly I would have gone home with him. But my homeland is now along the steep road of waiting to be handed over. Help me to stand against the winds as along as I have to, and not become tired. . . . Greetings and best wishes to the children. I bless you all each day, as long as I am able to give my blessing. May God protect everyone, and all the best to you.

With grateful greetings and wishes,

Alfred

To the Kreuser family, after January 21, 1945

Dear Friends,

For half the night I kept seeing in front of me the drawn and exhausted face of the faithful Tattenbach. Again and again I had to think about everyone who, in these hard times of test and trouble, is spending their strength and effort in order to help me. Since the guard has been sparing with the use of handcuffs today, I want to use the opportunity I've been given tonight to carry out a resolution: to thank all together everyone who is making an effort, just as every day with bound hands I send everyone my blessing, which is not fettered, and just as I think of everyone again and again during my nightly Mass and during the daily hours of waiting. If God in fact calls me home, one of my first requests to him will be for the friends who have passed the test of fidelity to God and have proved their love, to preserve that love from all danger. . . . I know from experience, friends, that today existence takes more than strength, and we've been affected and we're exhausted, and yet still there remains the mandatory call of love. So let's fail in anything except the thing that makes us human beings: adoration and love. Adoration and love: that's what it takes to be human. Thanks for all your loyalty and kindness and concern. There's an inner space where there's no evening and no farewell.

May God protect you. Good-bye.

Georg

CHAPTER 13

FINAL DAYS

January 23–February 2, 1945

On January 23, Delp's life in prison took a decisive turn: Helmuth von Moltke and Franz Sperr were taken to Plötzensee and hanged the same day. Executed with them were Nikolaus Gross and Theo Haubach, a socialist Kreisau member. (Writing to his wife, Moltke noted that he was dying "as a martyr for St. Ignatius of Loyola," and, in a final shot of humor, added that he shuddered at the thought of his deceased anti-Catholic father's reaction.)[1]

Delp was left totally alone now, the only Kreisau member whose fate still remained uncertain. And again: Why had he been passed over? Was there a sinister reason behind this decision? Was God making use of the delay to some unknown end? The anxiety was almost unbearable. In complete isolation now on his mountain cliff, he had come to the end of his physical and emotional strength. He had asked the Mariannes for more paper, hoping to take up again his reflections on the Litany of the Heart of Jesus, but his creativity too had become depleted. It took all his effort to cling to God minute by minute in an act of trust.

On the same day, January 23, a note from the Mariannes brought the news that ten days previously a son had been born to Ernst Kessler and his wife in Munich. They had named the baby Alfred Sebastian. Delp's mind may have returned fleetingly to the furtive message of warning from Kessler after his last Mass at St. Georg's all those many months ago. But what struck him most profoundly now was the contrast between the violence of the one act committed on this day and the miraculous wonder of the other—and yet, on some mysterious level, the close bond between the two: death and life.

He summoned up a reserve of strength to write a letter to the newborn. Then the reserve dried up and he had only a handful of lines left for those closest to him.

To Alfred Sebastian Kessler, January 23, 1945

Dear Alfred Sebastian,

Today, with great happiness and excitement, I received the news of your birth. Right away, with my bound hands, I sent you a big blessing. Since I don't know whether I'll ever see you in this life, I want to write you this letter, though I also don't know if it will ever reach you.

You've chosen a difficult time to begin your life. But that doesn't matter. A regular guy can handle anything. You have good parents who will certainly teach you how to deal with things.

And you've been given two good names. Alfred was a king who prayed a lot for his people, worked hard, and won many difficult battles. People didn't always understand him and so they often fought hard against him. Later they realized what he had done for his people and called him "Great." But the people of God called him "Saint." Before God and his fellow human beings he proved his worth. Sebastian was a courageous officer of both the emperor and God. But since the emperor didn't want to know anything about God, in his foolishness he fashioned sharp arrows of hate and mistrust, and gave leave to have the officer shot with them. Sebastian regained consciousness with a battered body but an unbroken spirit. He reproached the emperor for his foolishness, and for his honesty the emperor had him killed. But you'll be able to read about them later on, and your parents will have long since recounted the stories to you, dear little godchild. I want only to remind you that in your name lies an important obligation: that one must bear one's name with dignity and honor, courage and toughness, and that you must be steadfast if your name is to express the truth of your life.

And now, my dear one, I'd like to add still another burden to your name: a legacy. You also bear my name. And I'd like you to understand what I have wanted, just in case we don't become suitably acquainted with each other in this life; that is, the purpose to which I have placed my life—or better, to which it has been placed: to increase the praise and adoration of God; to help prove that people can live according to God's order and in the freedom of God, and that this is how to be human. I wanted to help, and want to help, find a way out of the great misery which we humans have gotten into and in which we have lost the right to be human. Only in adoration, in love, in living according to God's order, is a person free and capable of life. So here I've told you something of the insight and work and mission I desire for you.

Dear Alfred Sebastian, one must accomplish a lot in one's life. Flesh and blood alone can't manage it. If I were in Munich now, I'd be baptizing you one of these days—that is, I'd be giving you a share in the divine dignity to which we are all called. God's love, once in us, ennobles us and transforms us. We are from then on more than human beings. God's strength is at our disposal, God lives our life with us, and, my child, it should remain like this and become even more so. In this process also hangs the question of a person's final value. He becomes a person without price.

I'm living here on a very high mountain, dear Alfred Sebastian. What we tend to call life is far down, in a more hazy and confused darkness. Up here, human and divine solitude meet in serious dialogue. One must have clear eyes, otherwise one can't bear the light here. One must have good lungs, otherwise one can't breathe the air. One must be able to withstand heights, lonely narrow heights, otherwise one goes crashing down and becomes a victim of pettiness and deceit. Those are my desires for your life, Alfred Sebastian: clear eyes, good lungs, and the ability to reach and endure the free heights. I desire these not only for your physical progress and your external development and destiny, I desire much more that you live your life with God in adoration, in love, and in freely given service.

May almighty God bless and guide you, the Father, the Son, and the Holy Spirit.

Your godfather, Alfred Delp

I've written this with my hands in fetters; I'm not bequeathing these bound hands to you; rather, may freedom, which endures the fetters and in which one remains true to oneself, be given to you more beautifully, more tenderly, and more securely.

To Luise Oestreicher, January 23, 1945

Dear L.,

Today has been a really hard day. All my friends and companions are now dead, and I'm the only one left. The only one in fetters. I don't know what's behind this decision, but I'm assuming that it's not anything good. But perhaps it's the necessary connection to something firm.

I'm exhausted from sadness and fear. Humanly, it would have been easier to go with them. Life is taking strange routes before it releases me again onto this or that firm ground. I hope you all have a sense of how things are with me and are helping me through the days ahead by praying hard for me. On this same day, the day on which my friends have died, I got the news of the birth of little Alfred Sebastian. Death and life greet each other, and that's how it is.

More than ever, my life is standing absolutely on God. Every rational influence has been withdrawn. I pray and trust and surrender myself and rely on the Lord. I bless you and all my friends. Good-bye.

Georg

To Franz von Tattenbach, S.J., January 24, 1945

Dear Tatt,

Yesterday and today have been hard days. Helmuth and all the others have gone. I'm the only one left, the last one in "irons."

What does this mean? It's almost a confirmation and at the same time a terrible isolation. Probably the meaning is the clearly assumed one, but not the one you intended. But perhaps in this way I'll still have time. But why I without Helmuth? Is it an extended way of the cross? Or the connecting piece to firm ground? I can't write much today; I'm exhausted with sadness and also restlessness, despite all the trips across Lake Constance. It would probably have been easier to go with the others than to remain here, but this is how it is. And if there is to be a miracle, it would have to come this way. I hope you'll be stirred by good thoughts in order to pray hard for me in the days ahead.

Greetings to all my friends and acquaintances. Like yesterday, thanks and all protection and God's blessing. If only we could make world history run faster. We can certainly see where it's going. Why not a couple of weeks ahead of time? I'll see you again, one place or the other.

Bullus

To Marianne Hapig and Marianne Pünder, January 26, 1945

Good people,

This has been a hard week. The hardest of all, I think. Despite the apparent reference to my own way. Sometimes I'd really like to shut off for an hour. But even that isn't possible. As well, Buchholz has corrupted my imagination; right in the middle of my anguish over the others' deaths he told me exactly what happens when one is hanged. I think it would have been enough for me to experience it on the spot. Well, in any case, I know it now. And it wasn't a good time to find out about it.

Taking it in sips is harder on the heart. Please say nothing to Buchholz. But a person has to say some things once. That way, you get it off your chest. I now see no reasonable human beings the whole day.

Next week the First Friday, special to the Sacred Heart, and a Marian feast are on the same day. Please pray. Sunday's Mass is a prayer for all of us, and for me as well. Half of it is exactly true, and I hope the other half is true too.

I think that a lot depends on whether August can control his nerves and say nothing. Greetings to Pünder, please. I haven't forgotten him. Nor you yourselves and your concerns. God protect you all.

Your grateful Max

To Luise Oestreicher, January 26, 1945

Dear L.,

This week I've had the hardest and most miserable time since July. The death of friends, especially Helmuth, is truly bitter. As well, the experience of the logic of the disaster, so near and so cruel, the will to destruction, right up to the last. And then again this strange sensation of being left behind. I feel obligated again to live and hope. Although the obligation has not fallen as heavily on me as it has this week. The intention behind making me an exception isn't good. But God can use a bent stick to build a bridge over the marshland. I certainly don't need more.

It's too bad that communication is so difficult now. More than ever I would ask all of you to pray. But I know you're already there, helping me.

Don't worry so much; I've done enough now. Oh, if only I could shut off from time to time. But steadfastness is a virtue, and it becomes alive and real by in fact not shutting off.

All the best, dear one. And at the same time, a good Sunday. Only seventy days to Easter and the prayer, *pro tui nominis gloria misericorditer liberemur* [for the glory of your name may we be mercifully set free].[2] God bless you.

Georg

To Marianne Hapig and Marianne Pünder, January 30, 1945 (written on a prison order form)

Pray and have faith.
Thank you.

Dp

Plötzensee Prison

Although Alfred Delp's last written words were scratched on the prison order form sent to the Mariannes on January 30, his final act of faith may well have been expressed in the line from the Church's liturgy he had sent to Luise Oestreicher a few days earlier: "For the glory of your name may we be mercifully set free." It was his own personal experience of the classic Christian paradox and the one statement he had sought a few weeks earlier to sum up his own life.

On the morning of January 31, he heard the voice of the guard and then the harsh steely sound of the key unlocking his cell door. The police van carried him away from Tegel on the ten-minute ride to Plötzensee. There he was placed in cell 317, in the wing known as the House of the Dead. He was handed the striped shirt and trousers of the doomed prisoner, and an official form was placed before him on which were enumerated the articles he was leaving behind: one pair of trousers, one jacket, one pair of shoes, one winter overcoat, one hat, one pair of socks, one tie. . . . With an agitated hand he signed his name to the form.

A fellow prisoner who worked as a helper to the Catholic chaplain Peter Buchholz arranged for him to receive communion. When the prisoner visited Delp afterward, he saw a physical wreck of a man, his face pale and emaciated, his eyes sunken. He asked whether Delp would like something to read. Delp asked for *The Imitation of Christ.*

Two more days of waiting. On the afternoon of Friday, February 2, the feast of the Purification and a traditional day for Jesuits to make their vows, Buchholz was told that Delp would soon be executed. The chaplain went to cell 317. Inside, Delp, weakened from fear, struggle against despair, and a six-month preparation for death, still wondered if there might be hope of being saved from the rope. Could the Russian troops not get to Berlin in the next few minutes? Could world history not run faster? Buchholz had no answer. Delp's gaunt face then lit up with the playful smile of a child. "In half an hour," he said, "I'll know more than you do."[3]

The execution building was a short distance away. Walking upright, shoulders squared, and wearing the wooden shoes given to those about to be executed, Delp was led to the door of the building at about three o'clock in the afternoon. The execution formula was read out: "You have been sentenced by the People's Court to death by hanging. Executioner, do your duty."[4] The usual Plötzensee procedure was then no doubt followed: he was led forward, stripped to the waist, and guided under one of the hooks along a bar under the ceiling. The executioner, as likely as not fortified with brandy, placed a rope around his neck and hoisted him up. His prison pants were yanked off and his naked body struggled and twitched, then slackened, and then became still. The executioner made his routine pronouncement: "The sentence has been carried out."[5] Elsewhere in the prison, the form on which he had signed over his clothes was pulled from a pile and the date stamped in: *2 Feb. 1945.*

"For the glory of your name may we be mercifully set free."

The bodies of the condemned prisoners of Plötzensee were customarily burned; orders had been given after July 20 that the ashes of those implicated in the assassination plot be strewn over sewage waste. No record exists of exactly what happened to Delp's cremated remains, and it is presumed that they were disposed of in the same way as the ashes of all the others.

Later, a pair of broken eyeglasses, a rosary, and a copy of *The Imitation of Christ* were found in cell 317.

In an ironic coincidence rounding out Delp's life, the prisoners executed with him were Carl Goerdeler (who had been slated to become the chancellor of Germany, had a coup succeeded) and one of his more reactionary coresisters, Johannes Popitz—men from whom, in more optimistic days, Delp and Moltke had wanted to distance themselves because of divergent visions of a new society.

And yet another series of ironies: on the day of Delp's execution, Judge Roland Freisler condemned Dietrich Bonhoeffer's brother Klaus and his brother-in-law Rüdiger Schleicher to death. Then, on the following day, February 3, the air-raid siren sounded

The execution chamber at Plötzensee Prison. *Photo credit: Margaret Holubowich.*

just as yet another trial was beginning in the People's Court. As Freisler scrambled down the stairs, clutching the defendant's file, the building received a direct hit. The ceiling caved in and a beam fell on Freisler, crushing his skull. The doctor called in from the street who pronounced the judge dead was the brother of Rüdiger Schleicher. The defendant, crouching handcuffed in the basement, was Fabian von Schlabrendorff, a cousin of Dietrich Bonhoeffer's fiancée. Schlabrendorff was later acquitted of the charge of treason. The Gestapo never discovered that he had in fact tried to assassinate Hitler, having placed a bomb on Hitler's plane in March 1943 (the bomb failed to explode).

No official reason was ever given for the three-week delay in Delp's execution. His own surmise, that the Gestapo wanted to interrogate him and Augustin Rösch together, may have been correct. In prison, between severe beatings, Rösch had been threatened with the prospect of a face-to-face interrogation with Delp, his questioners chortling over the sport they would make of the spectacle. Rösch never came to trial, however, and he was freed when the Russian troops that Delp had longed for arrived in Berlin at the beginning of May. He became a director for the relief organization Caritas after the war and died in 1961. As for the Meier family, who had given Rösch refuge, four of the six sons had already been killed in combat by the time the family offered to hide the fugitive Jesuit. Of the four family members arrested with Rösch, the father, sixty-seven-year-old Wolfgang Meier Sr., died of typhus in Dachau six weeks later. Meier's daughter Maria was released after a week in prison, and his sons Wolfgang Jr. and Martin remained incarcerated in Dachau until the liberation of the camp in April.

The third Kreisau Jesuit, Lothar König, was never caught, in spite of widely circulated Gestapo bulletins that showed two photographs of him and one of Rösch. Ordered by Rösch to go into hiding, König had managed to escape from the Jesuit college in Pullach in late August 1944, just as two Gestapo officers were coming to arrest him. He was given refuge by friends near Starnberger See. In January 1945, after hearing of Rösch's arrest, he returned to Pullach under cover of darkness and hid in the coal shed of the Jesuit college until the American troops arrived in early May. His presence there was known to only one Jesuit brother. He became ill during these months of hiding, and, with medical care out of the question, his health deteriorated. After he emerged from the underground, he was diagnosed with cancer, and he died at the age of forty, a year after the war ended. In retaliation for the disappearance of the two Kreisau Jesuits, two other Jesuits were sent to Dachau, one from Munich and the other from Pullach. König's sister Ingeborg was imprisoned for the same reason. A third Jesuit was arrested at

St. Michael's Church in Munich for having helped one of his brother Jesuits to escape. All were liberated in the spring of 1945.

Immediately after the Jesuits received news of Delp's death, Tattenbach went to the Kreuser house to tell Maria Delp that her son had been executed. Before he could speak, she pleaded with him to take her to Berlin to see her son one last time. Courage left him at the sight of her anxious face, and Tattenbach left the house without breaking the news. Only on the third such attempt was he able to tell her what had happened to her son. Sometime later he also presented her with a suitcase containing Delp's clothes from prison. She kept the suitcase under her bed until her death in 1968.

The official notice of Delp's death, dated February 15, 1945, addressed to his mother, was received by Greta Kern in Lampertheim: "The clergyman Alfred Delp was sentenced to death by the People's Court of the Great German Reich. The sentence was carried out on February 2, 1945. The publication of a death notice is forbidden."

A public ritual marking Delp's death was not allowed, but, despite the injunction, a Mass for the Dead was celebrated at St. Georg's in early March. Delp's Bogenhausen friends gathered in grief. In future times, they would marvel that they had known a martyr and a hero of the German resistance. German streets and schools galore would be named after him. Stories would abound about him—about his big laugh, his cigar-chomping high-spiritedness, the way his face lit up in animated conversation, his skill as a handyman after bomb attacks, his ability to convert a sermon into an experience of prayer, the moving lines he had written from his prison cell. They would debate about how his life had turned out—that six months of imprisonment had transformed a rather unholy character into a saint; that, no, the transformation had begun long ago when he had decided, while struggling with his inner demons, to place God at the center of his life.

In future years, they would also find themselves in the midst of questions and controversy over Delp's writings: his thinking was prophetic and timeless; no, it was too nationalistic; his prison meditations provided a pattern by which one could live the Christian life; no, they were too pessimistic; they were too pious; not at all, they were (in the words of Thomas Merton) "perhaps the most clear-sighted. . . . Christian meditations of our time."[6] And his life: why were he and Rösch so much at odds with each other, and what were the real reasons for the delay of his final vows? Rösch, having survived the Nazi purge only to see Alfred Delp lionized and his own resistance work downplayed, was to make statements in future years that Delp's tendency to act independently had brought him dangerously close to the Hitler Youth at St. Blasien and had contributed to the actions that led to his arrest. Were there more skeletons in the closet?

An attempt to introduce Delp's cause for canonization a few decades later was soon to fizzle: the German Jesuits had spent their saint-making resources on Rupert Mayer, around whom an enormous following grew after his death in late 1945 (he was beatified in 1987). Mayer's case was straightforward; Delp's would have been complex and beset with stumbling blocks, much like the character of the man himself.

Questions would rage for decades from the comfortable standpoint of free speech and hindsight over who did what in the German resistance and whether any of it was enough. Were the Kreisau members simply a group of theorists and intellectuals dabbling in utopian dreams at a time when outright action was called for? There would even be debate over the moral courage of those who went to their deaths in Plötzensee, their acts of resistance against Nazism ignored by the Allies. And as for Catholic Church leaders—why were there not more stands taken? Why was the outrage not expressed more loudly? Nikolaus Gross, Delp's friend from Cologne, executed the same day as Moltke, was beatified by Pope John Paul II in October 2001 amid controversy: one of Gross's sons was reported as wanting nothing to do with his father's beatification because of Catholic officialdom's spotty track record during the Nazi era. And the controversies would continue. . . .

In March 1945 at the funeral Mass for Alfred Delp, however, all these questions and thoughts were matter for future consideration. Now, in the flattened city of Munich, in the tiny church of St. Georg, where the likeness of the saint faced the dragon's mouth, surrounded by pink-cheeked cherubs and gilt-edged curlicues, now, as the Mass for the Dead ended, Delp's friends rose and, in cracking voices, began to sing his favorite hymn.

And perhaps as they sang, they imagined him among them again—his eyeglasses somewhat askew, a crooked smile playing across his face, a cigar stub between his thumb and forefinger. And perhaps they could hear him booming along with them, his voice as blithely tuneless as ever, "Let us sing a song of joy. . . ."

EPILOGUE

Unlike much of Berlin, Plötzensee Prison survived the Allied bombing relatively intact. Today it continues to function as a prison, the sprawling drab brick compound now housing juvenile offenders. Huge keys still clank and grate in every door, metal against metal. The horrific Nazi connection, of course, is long past, except for one place that has been preserved as a *Gedenkstätte*, a memorial site. This is the low, cavernous, one-story brick building, where Alfred Delp and thousands of others were executed.

Inside the building, the cement floor and stark, dirty walls remain. The black curtain is now pulled to the side, revealing on the far wall two rounded windows crossed with thin iron bars. At first glance, the effect is shrinelike. But then: lined in front of the windows, along a high beam just below the ceiling, hang five giant meat hooks. Nausea wells up at the sight; the throat constricts.

A Jesuit priest who brings small groups to the site shakes his head, his face pained. This is a horrible place, he says, and the worst of it for him is the worry that his familiarity with it might breed indifference. Another group, another tourist stop.

Beneath my feet, the cement feels hard and cold as I stand looking down at a half-wilted wreath of flowers resting on the floor, then look up fleetingly at the row of hooks, then at the two church-style windows, and once again at the floor and the dusty flowers. At some point, perhaps only after I leave, I am reminded of Thomas More's words to his executioner, that the man was sending him, a condemned traitor, to God.[1]

For in fact, no matter how chilling this building is or how much one wants to turn away, it is a hallowed place, the ugly death hooks a paradox, a sign of contradiction. I think of those hundreds whose deaths here were seemingly senseless, those who normally kept their mouths shut and their eyes averted and in an unguarded moment were unlucky enough to be overheard speaking against the regime. Mostly, however, I think of those who actively chose to become part of what we now know as the German resistance, knowing full well that if they were found out, here was where they would end up.

In particular, I think of those I have come to admire above all: the Kreisau "friends," who, from disparate backgrounds and religious faiths, met in tiny apartments and cramped offices to plan for the future, and in the process came to a deeper understanding of what it means to live in human community and in Christian solidarity. I think of Peter Yorck von Wartenburg who wrote in his last letter to his wife, "May my death contribute just a little to reduce our present day's distance from God."[2] And Helmuth von Moltke's last written words to his wife: "You are my 13th chapter of the First Letter to the Corinthians. Without this chapter no human being is human."[3]

And I think of Alfred Delp, who wanted nothing more than, in his words as an eighteen-year-old, to "serve the Savior,"[4] and whose story and significance I have tried to unravel. These people and others like them, whose naked bodies hung down from these hooks like slabs of meat, came in touch with the mystery of God in the midst of the monstrous system they were struggling against. How can this not be a hallowed place, the cold cement floor holy ground?

After Nazism finally collapsed and the war ended, life moved on. The Marshall Plan came into effect and the massive work of restoring bombed-out Germany began. The Nuremberg trials took place in an effort to restore justice. The surviving German soldiers, having surrendered, returned to their families, among them Delp's two brothers, Ewald and Fritz, from American prisoner-of-war camps and his two remaining brothers-in-law from the front lines. His fellow Jesuits carried on in a fractured country, those in East Germany laboring under a new tyranny, those in West Germany taking some of the lead in Catholic theological renewal. The Jesuit journal *Stimmen der Zeit* resumed publication, eventually finding a home in a pleasant leafy suburb of Munich in a building named the Alfred Delp Haus. The carefully honed and hidden Kreisau documents were ignored, an anachronism in postwar Germany. "When I now read the texts, they don't seem very convincing to me," said Freya von Moltke more than fifty years after the documents were written. "They seemed of course marvelous at the time."[5]

And so as life goes on, what have they come to mean, these deaths? Where was God, it is asked, when the millions died in concentration camps? And, we might similarly ask, where was God when this group of upright people dreamed of a splendid renewal of humanity and planned for a just society in which human dignity would be respected and the things of God would be central? Where was God when it all came crashing down, their dreams and plans, and they landed in damp cells, their souls in anguish, their hands in chains, and, in the end, the remains of their bodies mingled with sewage waste?

No words can capture the realization that everything in your life has fallen to pieces, not only your external circumstances, but also your inner world, where pretense is no longer possible. "Wine-tinted dreams can fashion shapely jars from broken pots," writes Delp in his meditation on the prayer, "Come, Holy Spirit," "but sobriety soon shatters them," and sooner or later one is "faced with the naked truth and forced to make the age-old admission: I have wasted my substance."[6] Writing these lines with tied hands, shivering with hunger and the damp cold of his prison cell, facing his own death, he has already reached the bottom of the spiral into his own nothingness. He has been stripped little by little, realizing that God is not going to save him from feeling abandoned, and that, in fact, as things go from bad to worse, God allows him to be enveloped by darkness and incomprehension. Over and over again, he repeats the maxim of St. Teresa of Ávila, "God alone suffices," wanting to understand the truth of the words and, at the same time, wanting to recoil—and don't we all at one time or another?—but not being able to: facing four filthy walls, unable to move more than three paces this way and that, looking at a door that opens only from the outside. This is the place of Jesus on the Cross: "My God, my God, why have you forsaken me?" (Mark 15:34). "Oh, if only I could shut off from time to time," he writes in a letter of January 26, 1945. "But steadfastness is a virtue, and it becomes alive and real by in fact not shutting off."[7]

Helpless and alone, he slowly allows the terrifying vision of God to reveal itself. It is at this point, where one has fallen through to the bottom, where there are no comforts, where despair brings one close to annihilation, where one realizes the nothingness of one's life—this is where one enters the realm of God. Here is where trust and faith and love cease being mere words and become living realities.

This terrifying movement of the spirit is what prompted Thomas Merton to regard Alfred Delp's writings as those of a mystic.[8] "True mystical experience is nothing less than the shatteringly conscious awareness of [God's] continuous presence," Delp writes elsewhere in this same meditation, and one realizes that among his hours of terror and heart-weariness shone moments of this shattering awareness. He adds: "The Spirit of God is the supreme comforter because it overcomes finally and absolutely the fundamental sensations of misery and helplessness by driving the poison out of them."[9]

And in this rarified air of the mountaintop, as Delp described it, he was able to see the needs of humanity as a whole. He wrote as a patriotic German, his life deeply rooted in his own time and place, but underneath those particularities lies a profound understanding of the ills of humanity. The world continues to be plagued with war and injustice and corruption; the strong continue to triumph and the weak are pushed aside. State cruelty did not end with the Nazis; it has risen again and again, in the Soviet Union, in El Salvador, in Uganda, in Rwanda—the list is numbingly endless and goes back as far as human society itself. As a human race, we may yet destroy ourselves in one way or another. Alfred Delp's essential political message—if we lose our sense of God, we lose our understanding of what it is to be human—tends to be either ignored or twisted into self-serving ideology. It is not surprising that those with a similar message to his have all too often met his same earthly fate.

Nor does Delp excuse the Church. In fact, his comments are startling and devastating. "One thinks of all the meaningless attitudes and gestures—in the name of God? No, in the name of habit, of tradition, custom, convenience, safety, and even—let us be honest—in the name of middle-class respectability, which is perhaps the very least suitable vehicle for the coming of the Holy Spirit."[10]

And further, referring to the tendency to cloak dishonesty with pious words (an easy temptation in the Catholic Church, in which secrecy, power, and superficial piety too often are tightly interwoven): "At some future date the honest historian will have some bitter things to say about the contribution made by the churches to the creation of the mass-mind, of collectivism, dictatorships, and so on."[11] These words still ring true even in these post-Vatican II times and have been joined by other voices revealing fresh insights and challenges.

And yet perhaps there is something else at work here, something far more immense than the world's cruelty and godlessness, more powerful than the Church's failings, something of which we mortals can be given only the merest glimpse. "Our fate, no matter how much it may be entwined with the inescapable logic of circumstance," Delp writes, speaking of his own squalid situation, "is still nothing more than the way to God, the way the Lord has chosen for the ultimate consummation of his purpose."[12] Toward the end of one of his Christmas meditations, he speaks of steadfastness. At first glance, this seems a prosaic term, but in the context of ultimate choices it indicates the unwavering refusal to turn away from the horror of one's innate poverty. "Outwardly things are just as before and yet something has happened—there is a new consciousness of God's fatherly care in those who have stood the test of his questions."[13] To use a metaphor that he himself uses in referring to his final vows, the burning coal touches his lips and his life is transformed. His suffering is the doorway to God, his prison cell and bound hands the pathway to freedom. He has awakened to the realization that something infinitely greater is going on than his personal experience indicates. In that realization he surrenders himself to the mercy of God.

There will be moments ahead in the short time that Delp has left when despair returns—as it does for all of us—along with self-pity and rage and the whole range of attendant emotions. God does not take away these stultifying feelings any more than God reverses the suffering. Indeed, God may seem to act once again like an unprincipled thug, cutting one down at the knees and leaving one to bleed and die. And no one—not the saint, not the villain—escapes. But at the end, where one surrenders, there is grace.

This is why the execution chamber of Plötzensee, with its shrinelike windows and horrible butcher's hooks, is a holy place. In its mute starkness, it is a palpable connection with those who have been transformed through suffering. And in that connection lies the reminder that evil and human failing are not the last word, that every one of us somehow finally meets God at a point where the incomprehensible becomes clear and where, in mystery and paradox, failure triumphs.

NOTES

Prologue

1. Thomas à Kempis, *The Imitation of Christ* (London: Penguin Books, 1952), 87.

2. In the pre-Vatican II Church, First Fridays of the month were celebrated as days honoring the heart of Jesus. See page 205.

3. Roman Bleistein, *Alfred Delp: Geschichte eines Zeugen* (Frankfurt: Verlag Josef Knecht, 1989), 408.

4. See page 186.

Chapter 1
Young Scamp 1907–1926

1. Bleistein, *Alfred Delp,* 33.

2. Ibid., 34.

Chapter 2
Becoming a Jesuit 1926–1937

1. Roman Bleistein, *Begegnung mit Alfred Delp* (Frankfurt: Verlag Josef Knecht, 1994), 25–26.

2. Bleistein, *Alfred Delp,* 48.

3. Ibid., 70.

4. Helmuth James von Moltke, *Letters to Freya, 1939–1945* (New York: Alfred A. Knopf, 1990), 409.

5. Bernard A. Fiekers, Valkenburg Diary, 1935–1936, College of the Holy Cross archives, Worcester, Mass.

6. "Hitler Laws Affect Jesuits," *America,* vol. 54 (1935): 216.

7. Fiekers, *Valkenburg Diary.*

8. Bleistein, *Alfred Delp,* 416.

Chapter 3
War and Priestly Ministry 1937–1941

1. Walter Mariaux, trans., *The Persecution of the Catholic Church in the Third Reich: Facts and Documents* (New York: Longman, Green, 1942), 64.

2. "Papal Court Jester," *The Tablet* 241 (1987): 1248.

3. Bleistein, *Alfred Delp,* 139.

4. Ibid., 138.

5. Ibid., 141.

6. Alfred Delp, *Gesammelte Schriften,* vol. 1, *Geistliche Schriften* (Frankfurt: Verlag Josef Knecht, 1982), 278–79.

7. Bleistein, *Begegnung,* 23.

8. Lucia Simpson Shen, "A Martyr's Voice," *America* 152 (1985): 173.

9. A manuscript of about eighty pages with the title *Die Dritte Idee* (The Third Idea) was lost after Delp's arrest and has never been found.

10. Bleistein, *Alfred Delp,* 198.

11. Ibid., 196.

Chapter 4
The "Friends" of the Kreisau Circle 1941–1943

1. Roman Bleistein, *Augustinus Rösch: Leben im Widerstand* (Frankfurt: Verlag Josef Knecht, 1998), 305.

2. Moltke, 173.

3. Bleistein, *Alfred Delp,* 289.

4. Ibid., 200–201.

5. Moltke, 264.

6. Ibid.

7. Ibid., 277.

8. Ibid., 336.

9. Ibid.

Chapter 5
The Beginning of the End January–July 28, 1944

1. Bleistein, *Alfred Delp*, 420.

2. Ibid.

3. Moltke, 327.

4. Ibid., 255.

5. Bleistein, *Alfred Delp*, 297.

6. See page 189.

Chapter 6
Tegel Prison August–October 1944

1. Bleistein, *Alfred Delp*, 305.

2. See page 96.

Chapter 7
With Bound Hands October–November 1944

1. A reference to Moltke.

Chapter 8
Across the Abyss December 1–December 7, 1944

1. See page 93.

2. Delp, *The Prison Meditations of Father Alfred Delp* (New York: Herder & Herder, 1963), 21.

3. See page 205.

Chapter 9
Complete Surrender December 8–December 31, 1944

1. Delp, *Gesammelte Schriften,* vol. 4, *Aus dem Gefängnis,* 38.

2. From the Latin liturgy; the reference is to Isaiah 6:6.

3. Hosea 11:4.

4. Prayer of St. Ignatius of Loyola: "Take, Lord, and receive all my liberty, my memory, my understanding, and my entire will. Whatever I have and possess you have given all to me. To you, Lord, I now return it. All is yours. Dispose of it according to your will. Give me only your love and your grace; I will be rich enough; that is enough for me." From Mary Kathleen Glavich, S.N.D., *Handbook for Catholics* (Chicago: Loyola Press, 1995), 2.

5. Delp's vow formula document.

6. Sperr's street address in Munich.

7. This letter, dated December 16, was probably written a couple of months earlier.

8. The rest of this letter is illegible because of water damage.

9. The recipient of this letter is unknown; it was probably a fellow Jesuit.

10. Dr. Herman Pünder had been arrested in August and was acquitted by the People's Court on December 21, but he was then sent to Ravensbrück.

11. Reference to the trial of Herman Pünder.

12. A fifteenth-century German physician, natural scientist, and philosopher.

13. A sixteenth- and seventeenth-century mystic and philosopher.

14. Eugen Bolz, a politician who had been arrested after July 20 and was executed on January 23, 1945.

15. The prayer of Niklaus van der Flue, a fifteenth-century Swiss mystic: "My Lord and my God, take everything from me that hinders me from you; my Lord and my God, give me everything that carries me to you; my Lord and my God, take me from myself so that I might give myself entirely to you."

16. From the prayer *"Nada te turbe"* by St. Teresa of Ávila.

Chapter 10
Into the Fire January 1–January 8, 1945

1. Julius Langbehn, writer and cultural critic.

Chapter 11
Inferno January 9–January 11, 1945

1. Moltke, 400.

2. Bleistein, *Alfred Delp,* 377–78.

3. Ibid., 380–81.

4. Moltke, 402–3.

Chapter 12
After the Trial January 11–January 21, 1945

1. Bleistein, *Alfred Delp,* 392.

2. Delp, *Prison Meditations,* 137.

3. Ibid., 139.

4. Ibid.

5. Ibid., 179.

6. Marianne Junk, interview by author, Fulda, Germany, 27 May 2000.

Chapter 13
Final Days January 23–February 2, 1945

1. Moltke, 404.

2. From the prayer for Septuagesima Sunday, which was seventy days before Easter on the pre-Vatican II Church calendar.

3. Bleistein, *Alfred Delp,* 408.

4. Ibid., 409.

5. Ibid.

6. Thomas Merton, *Turning Toward the World,* vol. 4, *The Journals of Thomas Merton* (San Francisco: HarperSanFrancisco, 1996), 249.

Epilogue

1. This reference is to *A Man for All Seasons,* by Robert Bolt.

2. Marion Yorck von Wartenburg, *The Power of Solitude: My Life in the German Resistance* (Lincoln, Nebr.: University of Nebraska Press, 2000), 91.

3. Moltke, 411.

4. See page 6.

5. Freya von Moltke, interview by author, Norwich, Vt., 30 July 2000.

6. Delp, *Prison Meditations,* 151.

7. See page 206.

8. Thomas Merton, introduction to *The Prison Meditations of Father Alfred Delp,* by Alfred Delp (New York: Herder & Herder, 1963), xxvii.

9. Delp, *Prison Meditations,* 145.

10. Ibid., 87.

11. Ibid., 114.

12. Ibid., 31.

13. Ibid., 68.

BIBLIOGRAPHY

Andreas-Friedrich, Ruth. *Berlin Underground, 1938–1945*. Translated by Barrows Mussey. New York: Paragon House, 1947.

Balfour, Michael, and Julian Frisby. *Helmut von Moltke: A Leader against Hitler*. London: Macmillan, 1972.

Beevor, Antony. *The Fall of Berlin, 1945*. London: Viking Penguin, 2002.

Bleistein, Roman. *Alfred Delp: Geschichte eines Zeugen*. Frankfurt: Verlag Josef Knecht, 1989.

———. *Augustinus Rösch: Leben im Widerstand*. Frankfurt: Verlag Josef Knecht, 1998.

———. *Begegnung mit Alfred Delp*. Frankfurt: Verlag Josef Knecht, 1994.

———. *Die Jesuiten im Kreisauer Kreis*. Passau, Germany: Wissenschaftsverlag Richard Rothe, 1990.

Boehm, Eric. *We Survived: Fourteen Histories of the Hidden and Hunted of Nazi Germany*. Santa Barbara, Calif.: Clio Press, 1966.

Conway, John S. *The Nazi Persecution of the Churches, 1933–45*. Toronto: Ryerson Press, 1968.

Delp, Alfred. *Gesammelte Schriften*. 5 vols. Frankfurt: Verlag Josef Knecht, 1984.

———. *The Prison Meditations of Father Alfred Delp*. New York: Herder & Herder, 1963.

Dietrich, Donald J. *Catholic Citizens in the Third Reich*. New Brunswick, N.J.: Transaction Books, 1988.

Fest, Joachim. *Plotting Hitler's Death.* New York: Henry Holt, 1996.

Guibert, Joseph de. *The Jesuits: Their Spiritual Doctrine and Practice.* Chicago: The Institute of Jesuit Sources, 1964.

Guttenberg, Elisabeth von. *Holding the Stirrup.* New York: Little, Brown, 1952.

Hamerow, Theodore S. *On the Road to the Wolf's Lair.* Cambridge, Mass.: Harvard University Press, 1997.

"Hitler Laws Affect Jesuits." *America* 54 (1935): 216.

Hoensbroech, Paul von. *Fourteen Years a Jesuit.* Translated by Alice Zimmem. London: Cassell, 1911.

Hoffman, Peter. *The History of the German Resistance, 1933–1945.* Translated by Richard Barry. Montreal: McGill-Queen's University Press, 1996.

Kempis, Thomas à, *The Imitation of Christ.* Translated by Leo Sherley-Price. London: Penguin, 1952.

Kulka, Otto Dov, and Paul R. Mendes-Flohr, eds. *Judaism and Christianity under the Impact of National Socialism.* Jerusalem: The Historical Society of Israel and the Zalman Shazar Center for Jewish History, 1987.

Lapomarda, Vincent A. *The Jesuits and the Third Reich.* Lewiston, N.Y.: Edwin Mellen Press, 1989.

Lewy, Guenter. *The Catholic Church and Nazi Germany.* New York: McGraw-Hill, 1964.

MacDonogh, Giles. *A Good German: Adam von Trott zu Solz.* Woodstock, N.Y.: Overlook Press, 1992.

Mariaux, Walther, trans. *The Persecution of the Catholic Church in the Third Reich: Facts and Documents.* New York: Longman, Green, 1942.

Merton, Thomas. *Turning Toward the World.* Vol. 4, *The Journals of Thomas Merton.* Edited by Victor A. Kramer. San Francisco: HarperSanFrancisco, 1996.

———. Introduction to *The Prison Meditations of Father Alfred Delp,* by Alfred Delp. New York: Herder & Herder, 1963.

Micklem, Nathaniel. *National Socialism and the Roman Catholic Church.* London: Oxford University Press, 1939.

Moltke, Helmuth James von. *Letters to Freya, 1939–1945.* New York: Alfred A. Knopf, 1990.

"Papal Court Jester." *The Tablet* 241 (1987): 1118, 1238.

Phayer, Michael. *The Catholic Church and the Holocaust, 1930–1965.* Bloomington: Indiana University Press, 2000.

———. *I Remember.* Translated by Harvey D. Egan. New York: Crossroad, 1985.

———. *Karl Rahner in Dialogue.* New York: Crossroad, 1986.

Reck-Malleczewen, Friedrich. *Diary of a Man in Despair.* Translated by Paul Rubens. London: Duckworth Literary Entertainments, 2000.

Roon, Ger van. *German Resistance to Hitler: Count von Moltke and the Kreisau Circle.* Translated by Peter Ludlow. London: Van Nostrand Reinhold, 1971.

Rürup, Reinhard, ed. *Topography of Terror.* Berlin: Verlag Willmuth Arenhövel, 1989.

Sánchez, José M. *Pius XII and the Holocaust.* Washington, D.C.: The Catholic University of America Press, 2001.

Schlabrendorff, Fabian von. *The Secret War against Hitler.* Translated by Hilda Simon. New York: Pitman, 1965.

Scholl, Inge. *The White Rose: Munich 1942–1943.* Translated by Arthur R. Schultz. Middletown, Conn.: Wesleyan University Press, 1983.

Shen, Lucia Simpson. "A Martyr's Voice," *America* 152 (1985): 171–73.

Speaight, Robert. *Teilhard de Chardin: A Biography.* London: Collins, 1967.

Tyrell, George. *Christianity at the Crossroads.* London: George Allen & Unwin, 1909.

Vassiltchikov, Marie. *The Berlin Diaries, 1940–1945.* London: Methuen London, 1985.

Yorck, Marion von Wartenburg. *The Power of Solitude: My Life in the German Resistance.* Lincoln, Nebr.: University of Nebraska Press, 2000.

Video Recordings

The Eye of the Dictator. Directed by Hans-Günther Stark. Written and produced by Terry Stratton-Smith. 55 min. Distributed by Charisma Films Ltd., London, England, 1994. Videocassette.

Traitors against Hitler. Distributed by Deutsche Reportagefilm, Bonn, Germany, 1969.

Unpublished Documents

Fiekers, Bernard A. Valkenburg Diary. College of the Holy Cross archives, Worcester, Mass.

Lasst Uns dem Leben Trauen: P. Alfred Delp (1907–1945). Private memorial booklet, Christmas 1996.

Walsh, Edmund A. *Papers.* College of the Holy Cross archives, Worcester, Mass.

INDEX